AUTISM

The Continuum Counseling Series

AUTISM

A Practical Guide for Those Who Help Others

John Gerdtz
and
Joel Bregman, M.D.

Foreword by William Van Ornum

Continuum | *New York*

1990

The Continuum Publishing Company
370 Lexington Avenue
New York, NY 10017

Copyright © 1990 by John Gerdtz and Joel Bregman, M.D.
Foreword Copyright © 1990 by William Van Ornum

Printed in the United States of America

Library of Congress Cataloging-in-Publication Data

Gerdtz, John.
    Autism : a practical guide for those who help others / John Gerdtz
and Joel Bregman ; foreword by William van Ornum.
        p.   cm. — (The Continuum counseling series)
    Includes bibliographical references.
    ISBN 0-8264-0462-6
    1. Autism. 2. Autism—Social aspects. I. Bregman, Joel.
II. Title. III. Series.
RJ506.A9G47   1990
616.89'82—dc20   89-71247
                                                              CIP

Contents

85476

Foreword

The Continuum Counseling Series–the first of its kind for a wide audience–presents books for everyone interested in counseling, bringing to readers practical counseling handbooks that include real-life approaches from current research. The topics deal with issues that are of concern to each of us, our families, friends, acquaintances, or colleagues at work.

General readers, parents, teachers, social workers, psychologists, school counselors, nurses and doctors, pastors, and others in helping fields too numerous to mention will welcome these guidebooks that combine the best professional learnings and common sense, written by practicing counselors with expertise in their specialty.

Increased understanding of ourselves and others is a primary goal of these books–and greater empathy is the quality that all professionals agree is essential to effective counseling. Each book offers practical suggestions on how to "talk with" others about the theme of the book, be this in an informal and spontaneous conversation or in a more formal counseling session.

Professional therapists will value these books also, because each volume in The Continuum Counseling series develops its subject in a unified way, unlike many other books that may be either too technical or, as edited collections of papers, may come across to readers as being disjointed. In recent years both the American Psychological Association and the American Psychiatric Association have endorsed books that build on the scientific traditions of each profession but are communicated in an interesting way to general readers. We hope that professors and students in fields such as psychology, social work, psychiatry, guidance and counseling, and other helping fields will find these books to be helpful companion readings for undergraduate and graduate courses.

From nonprofessional counselors to professional therapists, from students of psychology to interested lay readers, The Continuum Counseling Series endeavors to provide informative, interesting, and useful tools for everyone who cares about learning and dealing more effectively with these universal, human concerns.

Autism

Autism is a rare phenomenon, and despite events such as the appearance of Dustin Hoffman in the movie *Rain Man,* much of the public as well as professionals themselves are unaware of the many advances being made to help people with autism. And the Hoffman character was not a representative example of what it is like to be a person with autism. Although a sense of the separateness and alienation was conveyed, *Rain Man* was the story of an autistic person with some very special "savant" skills. But autism encompasses more than Dustin Hoffman's "Rain Man" character. John Gerdtz brings to readers of The Continuum Counseling Series a highly informative as well as comprehensive portrayal of facts about, and approaches toward, autism, and his colleague Joel Bregman, M.D., of Yale University, presents a current view toward the biopsychiatric factors involved in autism.

This is a book that gives us an understanding of the many issues connected with autism over the past fifty years. The diagnosis itself and theories about its causes prompted many battles in professional circles. Gerdtz outlines these in his description of "The Autism Wars." For a time some espoused the view that autism is caused by a particularly cold and distant kind of parenting. Now this hypothesis has been left behind in favor of the view of autism as a genetic and biochemical condition. Nevertheless, the overall functioning of the brain remains a great mystery and there are many frontiers left to explore.)

Not only do we learn about autism, readers will learn about the many practical things that can be done to help the individual and his family. Gerdtz recognizes that families are systems and that any interventions done can have an effect on the entire system. Throughout the book there is a highly compassionate and well-informed emphasis on how to help families with a member who has autism. This could have only been written by someone who has listened to families and learned so many lessons from them that he is able to pass these learnings on to others. And there is humility—writes Gerdtz: "Yet much about autism is still unknown, so much of what we think of autism is probably wrong, and there are still tremendous gaps in services."

As I read through this book I was impressed by John Gerdtz's interest in, and advocacy for, the person with autism. There is an excellent discussion of Public Law 94-142, which mandates free and appropriate educational services for all handicapped students. Parents and those who work with families such as counselors, social workers, and educators will find this a highly worthwhile chapter. There are many valuable services available today, although these services have outpaced the information available about them. (Gerdtz points out that he has seen some cases where students were kept at home for over a year because the educational and human services network could not find an appropriate placement. He is a strong advocate for these youngsters in those situations "where children with autism or other handicapping conditions simply do not receive the educational services that they are guaranteed by law.")

A theme throughout the book is that every person with autism is unique and that we must try everything in order to help these people. Gerdtz is particularly impressed with much of the fine behavioral research that emphasizes the development of specific social skills and life skills. However, he reminds us that since so much is currently unknown about autism, it is best to keep an open mind toward any approach that might be helpful to lessen the suffering of these people.

Counselors themselves may wonder, "What do I say when working with the families?" "Can autistic people themselves benefit from counseling?" "Are there national organizations that can assist?" Gerdtz answers these questions and others.

Every chapter includes a detailed reference list, indicative of the latest research in the field, and much of this comes from the work of Gerdtz's colleagues at Yale University and the Benhaven School. There is a particular note of enthusiasm when Gerdtz discusses "supported employment," of providing meaningful jobs in the community for people with autism.

Joel Bregman's chapter addresses the important concerns connected with using medication as a treatment for autism. This is a significant contribution because it emphasizes the wide range of different medications currently in use, and addresses some of the side effects that must be carefully watched for when these are prescribed.

This is a book to inform parents, family members, and the many professionals who work with them. It provides hope that every person with autism can be helped to be a fuller participant in and contributor to society. The scientific research of over fifty years is brought in to be a foundation for a range of practical interventions. This volume could only have been written with an intimate knowledge of autism and those who suffer from it. Gerdtz succeeds in conveying the many ways that people with autism are similar to ourselves, despite whatever seemingly strange symptoms they may express.

John Gerdtz has worked with several fine programs that serve people with autism. The most current, Benhaven, is an internationally recognized center that was started by a parent over twenty years ago so that her son Ben could have a safe place to grow—hence the name Benhaven: Ben's Haven. The knowledge from this book will help families and their helpers to create other "havens" so that people who have autism will be able to grow and live at their full potential.

William Van Ornum, Ph.D.
Marist College
Poughkeepsie, New York

General Editor
The Continuum Counseling Series

1

Basic Questions about Autism

Charles N. was brought to me by his mother on February 2, 1943, at four years of age, with the chief complaint, "The thing that upsets me the most is that I can't reach my baby."

—Report by Leo Kanner, M.D. (1985)
first published in 1943.

Sometimes he looks right through me, as if I'm not there.
—Mother of preschool boy, 1988.

I am happy when I clean houses
I am sad when I clean floors
I am happy when I listen to music.
—Statement written by young adult.

We lead a life of uneasy ambivalence. Some days we search for miracle cures, other days we celebrate the everyday miracles: support from those who love us, teachers who are amazingly caring and understanding, gifted and compassionate doctors who don't make us wait in waiting rooms. It is these everyday miracles that sustain us on darker days. . . . And the next time you pass a house with a little boy staring out the window, stop and wave.
—From "Rain Boy" by Patricia A. Dreier,
parent of a young boy with autism,
in the *New York Times* (Feb. 19, 1989).

All of the statements above were by or about a person diagnosed as autistic. There has been great progress in services for children and adults with autism over the past forty-five years. Yet so much is still unknown, so much of what we think we know about autism is probably wrong, and there are still tremendous gaps in the services many people with autism and their families need.

The essential component in any understanding of autism is the realization that people with autism are people first. Individuals with autism differ in their personalities, needs, and desires as much as any other group of people. Although we know in general which approaches are most likely to be successful in programs for people with autism, there is not a single best educational strategy, behavior modification program, medication, or therapy for all autistic children and adults. Working in this field requires a constant willingness to adjust and adapt theories and interventions to the needs of individual people and situations, an ability to observe and listen to what the person with autism and his/her family have to say about his/her situation, and the flexibility to evaluate systematically what you are doing, and change your approach where necessary.

People frequently ask me for information about autism. Some of the most common questions are listed below.

What Is Autism? Is It Some Kind of Disease?

Autism is not a disease. It is both a behavioral syndrome and a developmental disability. Autism as a behavioral syndrome means that people with autism frequently display certain clusters of behaviors that distinguish them from those who are not autistic. There are four broad categories of behavior consistent with the diagnosis of autism (adapted from Cohen, Paul, and Volkmar, 1987, p. 30).

(1) Difficulties with social relationships

People with autism relate to other people in a very strange manner. They may completely ignore other people in the environment, or they may attempt to make social contact in bizarre ways such as touching, pulling at, or sniffing other people. Children and adults with autism frequently have significant problems in expressing emotions appropriately, or developing any understanding of the emotions of others. A person with autism often does not form emotional attachments to people in his/her life in the same way as a nonautistic person. The autistic person may be equally affectionate with familiar people (family members) as with complete strangers. Some people with autism appear to be equally attached to an object (for example a blanket) as they are to familiar people in their environment. These strange behaviors and lack of ordinary social skills do not mean that the autistic person is totally indifferent to other people. Autistic children are usually very attached to their parents and other family members, and adults with autism also have people around them who become very important to them. It is the inability to understand and develop the basic give-and-take of ordinary social relationships with a variety of people that is the basic characteristic of the behavioral syndrome of autism.

(2) Severe deficits in language

About half of all people with autism remain nonverbal (mute) all their lives (Wing and Attwood, 1987, p. 6). Those who develop speech often have unusual ways of speaking. Some autistic people speak in a strange mechanical monotone, others reverse pronouns, or are echolalic (constantly repeating a word or phrase that another person has used), or use verbal language in other bizarre ways. Children with autism may develop speech later than nonhandicapped children, or in certain cases, the autistic child may develop speech normally, only to lose this ability later.

(3) Severe deficits in communication

This is related to the autistic person's difficulty in developing social relationships: there are often significant problems in initiating and responding to the verbal and nonverbal aspects of communication. The person with autism usually has problems understanding the "body language" of others, how to start and end a conversation, how to take turns during conversation, how close to stand when speaking to others, etc.

(4) Other associated features

Generally at least one of these features is part of the syndrome of autism, although many people with autism will display a number of features.

i. Strong resistance to change in the environment
The person with autism may respond emotionally, and sometimes violently, to relatively minor changes in the environment. These changes could include an alteration in the furniture arrangement in a room, different clothing, moving to another bedroom, being transported in an unfamiliar vehicle, etc.

ii. Insistence on a routine
Most people with autism insist on a stable routine for doing many things. If there is a change in routine, for whatever reason, there can be a very strong reaction. For many people with autism there is no such thing as a "good" surprise; any change in the regular way of doing things is bad.

iii. Odd movements

Some people with autism consistently display unusual body movements. The most common types of movements include rocking back and forward while seated, toe walking, prolonged twirling or spinning movements in the hands or fingers, spinning the body in circles, rhythmic rocking from one foot to another while standing.

iv. Behavior problems

A minority of the autistic population develops severe problem behaviors including self-injury (hitting or biting self, head banging), destruction of property, and assaulting others. These behaviors can be triggered by a wide variety of factors and circumstances, including unexpected changes in schedule or routine, frustration and anger, as a way of communicating fear, anxiety, or boredom or other emotions.

v. Attachment to inanimate objects

In some cases, a child or adult with autism will become attached to a certain inanimate object for a prolonged period of time. If the object is lost or removed, the autistic person may become angry or upset. People with autism may be so preoccupied with an object that they twirl or spin the object for hours, and strongly resist any attempt to redirect them from this activity.

vi. Very unusual responses to common stimuli in the environment

Commonplace sights, sounds, or smells in the environment may be intensely exciting to a person with autism. Some people with autism spend considerable time staring at certain types of lights, drumming objects on hard surfaces, rubbing favored surfaces or textures, etc.

vii. Lack of imaginative play

The child or adult with autism is usually very concrete and focused on the here and now in his/her thinking and play. People with autism are often very limited in their ability to pretend, or to use their imagination to describe situations or manipulate toys. A study comparing the symbolic or imaginative play of children with both autism and severe mental retardation with the play of a group of children with just severe mental retardation (Wing, Gould, Yates, and Brierley, 1985), found that the autistic children generally had very little ability in the area of imaginative play. Most of the children with autism played in a very repetitive isolated manner, while the other children, who were severely handicapped but not autistic, had developed a variety of imaginative play activities. This lack of symbolic play can be a significant deficit. There is evidence that the development of imaginative and symbolic play is an important foundation for the development of many other important cognitive, social, and language skills (Groden and Groden, 1985; Wing et al., 1985, pp. 327– 28).

viii. The presence of "splinter skills"
People with autism sometimes have certain skills that are very well developed, although they may be severely handicapped in general. In contrast, people who are mentally retarded, but not autistic, usually have a more even pattern of intellectual development (Autism Society of North Carolina, 1989, p. 4).

Autism occurs along a continuum. One end of the continuum includes people with autism who are severely or profoundly mentally retarded and need constant care and support, while at the other end are people of above average intelligence with college degrees or higher levels of formal education who live independently in their own homes. Over 70 percent of the people diagnosed as autistic are also mentally retarded (Lerea, 1987, p. 277), so that the great majority of autistic people need some kind of ongoing support and training for life.

In addition to being a behavioral syndrome, autism is also a developmental disability. This means that the person with autism is likely to be disabled to some extent for life. Autism is usually diagnosed by the time a child is three years old, and will almost certainly be diagnosed before a person reaches adulthood. People with autism change as they develop, as do all people, but the person who receives an appropriate diagnosis of autism is likely to remain autistic for life (Cohen, Paul, and Volkmar, 1987, pp. 30–31).

Virtually everyone in our society has, at one time or another, probably exhibited some of the behaviors associated with autism. Naturally, this does not mean that a person is autistic. For an appropriate diagnosis of autism, the behaviors have to be severe, prolonged, and from all four of the categories described above. Even if this criterion is met, it is not always easy to make a diagnosis of autism. The autism diagnosis should only be made by an appropriately trained and experienced professional, who is familiar with the syndrome of autism, and who uses the proper standardized assessment instruments as part of the diagnostic process. Diagnosis will be discussed more fully in a following question.

How Is Autism Diagnosed?

Professional disputes about the most appropriate method to diagnose autism have persisted since Leo Kanner first reported the syndrome in 1943: some of these disputes continue today (Cohen, Paul, and Volkmar, 1987, pp. 20–21). But there is now much more of a consensus among those in the field of autism as to diagnosis than in the past.

A formal diagnosis of autism is usually done by a psychiatrist or properly licensed psychologist who is familiar with autism and other developmental disabilities. The diagnosis should be based on direct observations of the person for whom a diagnosis is being requested, as well as interviews with parents, family members, and other important people in the person's life. A detailed life history should be part of any diagnostic procedure. Most professionals will follow a systematic method of diagnosis such as that provided in the *Diagnostic and Statistical Manual (DSM)* of the American Psychiatric Association.

If further information is needed for a diagnosis of autism there are standardized instruments that may be helpful. These instruments include the Childhood Autism Rating Scale (CARS) and the Autism Screening Instrument for Educational Planning (ASIEP). The CARS (Schopler, Reichler, and Renner, 1986) and the ASIEP (Krug, Arick, and Almond, 1980), are useful not only in developing goals and objectives for educational and training programs for people with autism, but can also be used in the process of distinguishing autism from other handicapping conditions (Teal and Wiebe, 1986).

There are cases where even skilled and experienced professionals will disagree concerning a definite diagnosis of autism (Sugiyama and Abe, 1989). In these cases it is best to follow up with another professional, or team of professionals, in order to arrive at a conclusive diagnosis. Conflicting diagnoses contribute to family stress (Donnellan and Mirenda, 1984), and make it difficult to plan an appropriate educational or rehabilitation program (see Lerea, 1987, for a comprehensive discussion of diagnosis and assessment in autism).

What Are People with Autism Like?

Children and adults with autism have individual personalities just like everyone else. Individuals with autism vary greatly in their intellectual capacity, social skills, and ability to cope with the everyday demands of society. A common factor in the lives of all people with autism, even those with above normal intelligence living relatively independently in the community, is a difficulty with social relationships and the use of language (Paul, 1987, p. 126).

Lorna Wing (Wing and Attwood, 1987), a leading researcher in autism, identified three major types of social interactions in the autistic population. The three types are: the aloof group, the passive group, and the active but odd group. These are not rigid categories of people, and the same individual may move from one group to another over time, or when faced with different circumstances (Wing and Attwood, 1987, p. 5). The characteristics of the groups are summarized below, but for further information the reader should see Wing and Attwood (1987).

The aloof group

As implied in the title, people in the aloof group tend to reject physical and social contact with others. Although persons in this group may enjoy some brief periods of physical comforting or play, they usually abruptly move on to some other activity when they have experienced sufficient physical contact. As infants and toddlers, members of the aloof group rarely show the type of attachment behavior that a nonhandicapped or mentally retarded child would exhibit toward his/her parents. Naturally, most parents find this behavior distressing and incomprehensible.

Members of the aloof group tend to be nonverbal and remain so for life. If they develop speech their verbal skills are usually very limited, and may be limited to single words or simple phrases. People in the aloof group will spend hours in solitary, repetitive activities, and be very dependent on schedules and routines. This group seems to have the most behavior problems of the three groups, including bizarre noises and gestures, temper tantrums, self-injury, assault, and property destruction, although only a relatively small minority of the group will show these behaviors on a severe or frequent basis. At times, the behaviors may be brought on by a change or interruption in routine, at other times there may be no apparent cause.

The passive group

Members of this group seem to be less resistant to social and physical contact than the aloof group. People in the passive group will take part in some group activities, although they will rarely seek out social contact. The passive group is also generally caught up in routines and schedules, but will react less strongly than the aloof group if the routines are interrupted. Although passive group people can exhibit problem behaviors, these behaviors tend to be of a lesser intensity and severity than in the aloof group.

Because of a general willingness to "go along" with what is happening in their environments, people in the passive group usually fit in well in a variety of educational and training programs, while members of the aloof and active but odd groups are more likely to need special programs for individuals with autism.

The active but odd group

This group is in many ways the opposite extreme of the aloof group. Members of this group are more likely to develop speech than the members of the other groups, and may demonstrate extensive vocabularies. Although the onset of speech may be delayed as compared with nonhandicapped children, some members of this group may begin speaking in complete sentences very soon after they first develop speech: however, the speech usually sounds mechanical or strange in some way. People in this group generally share the need for routine and structure exhibited by the other two groups. There is also the possibility that certain behavior problems may be exhibited. An interesting characteristic of the active but odd group is that the people in the group often find a single interest in such things as dates and calendars, staff schedules, certain types of people, types of automobiles, etc., and that this interest is "pursued so relentlessly, to the exclusion of virtually everything else, and with little grasp of the meaning or applicability to everyday life of the knowledge acquired" (Wing and Attwood, 1987, p. 10).

People in this group will often, with single-minded determination, approach complete strangers and ask a single question over and over, or launch a barrage of questions about a favored topic. Some of the members of this group may respond with anger or temper tantrums if their questions are cut off or the "right" answer is not given.

The active but odd group does not fit the common concept of autism, and a diagnosis of autism may not be given because the person is so "sociable." But this sociability is usually very much a one-way street, and the contacts that the active but odd person makes do not form the basis of the give-and-take of most social interactions. Members of the active but odd group are people who "have enough language and symbolic development to take in something of the environment, but not enough to make a coherent whole of their experience" (Wing and Attwood, 1987, p. 11).

It is important to remember that the three groups of aloof, passive, and active but odd are not rigid categories in the autistic population. As noted above, an individual with autism could have the characteristics of all three groups at different times in his/her growth and development. Wing suggests that it is possible to assign people to one of these groups, based on his/her primary mode of social interaction at one particular time, with the understanding that the assignment may change at a different time or in a different circumstance. According to Wing, the best time to evaluate mode of social interaction is when the person with autism sees a stranger for the first time, or that person's relations with other persons during un-structured times (Wing and Attwood, 1987, p. 11).

With all the descriptions of lack of social contact, problems with language, need for structure and routine, and possible behavior problems, people with autism can sound almost pathologically self-centered, or like someone from another planet. It is not that the child or adult with autism has chosen to be isolated or completely wrapped up in routines and schedules, but that this is the only way he/she is able to make any sense of reality and the demands of the environment. Other people are very important to people with autism. Although the characteristics and symptoms must be described, it is easy to forget that there is a real person trying to make some kind of contact under all those behaviors. Sometimes the contact is made and a kind of relationship with a parent, brother or sister, teacher or other staff member, neighbor or fellow worker, slowly and painfully starts to grow. It should not be forgotten that the autistic person's need for structure and routine can also be the basis for effective teaching, job training, and employment (Lerea, 1987).

Are Many People with Autism Like the Character Played by Dustin Hoffman in the Movie *Rain Man*?

Rain Man led to a tremendous increase in the public awareness of autism. The character Dustin Hoffman portrayed so expertly would be considered an autistic savant. Savants are people with extraordinary skills in a certain area such as music, art, mathematics, memorization, etc., although the person has never received formal training or education in the skilled area. Savant skills are especially remarkable in people who may otherwise be severely handicapped and need help in coping with the demands of daily life.

About 10 percent of children and adults with autism have savant skills, but more than half those who are savants have two or more special skills. Savant skills are more common in autism than in other disability groups (Blake, 1989, p. 1). How or why certain people develop savant skills is still a matter of some debate, and it is unlikely that one simple explanation of this phenomenon will be found. There seems to be evidence that some savant skills are inherited, while other studies suggest certain environmental factors in addition to specific types of brain injury (see Blake, 1989, for a good discussion of savants).

One of the less-desirable effects of the movie was the public perception that all people with autism have some kind of remarkable savant skill. It is possible to spend most of one's career in the field of autism and not meet a savant. After *Rain Man* was released, many schools and other programs for autistic children and adults received calls from television and newspaper reporters. The reporters wanted to find another Rain Man. Many of the reporters were dismayed to learn that most people with autism are not savants, and the reporters had little further interest in the topic of autism. I felt this was an unfortunate reaction. There are fascinating stories about children and adults with autism who are not savants. I remembered the ten-year-old boy with autism and severe mental retardation who, after a year, was able to order lunch at a fast-food restaurant by pointing to pictures on a communication board: his story had, in its own way, as much drama, courage, and determination as did *Rain Man*.

Is Autism Very Common?

Autism is a fairly rare condition, and is certainly less common than some other developmental disabilities such as mental retardation. Estimates for the prevalence of autism in various populations have varied considerably, often due to disagreements as to how to appropriately diagnose the syndrome (Zahner and Pauls, 1987). A number of more recent epidemiological surveys of autism in a variety of countries indicate that about two people per ten thousand in the general population could be considered as autistic using conservative methods of diagnosis (Zahner and Pauls, 1987, pp. 202–3): this estimate could rise to about four or five people per ten thousand if broader categories of diagnosis were used. Other researchers have even higher estimates of the prevalence of autism (Sugiyama and Abe, 1989) in certain areas.

The surveys also indicated that autism was more common in males than in females, although the ratio of the sexes varied from survey to survey (Zahner and Pauls, 1987, pp. 203–4), with a range of ratios 3:1 or 4:1 males to females.

Autism is found around the world (Everard, 1987), in all racial and ethnic groups, as well as in all socioeconomic classes (Zahner and Pauls, 1987, pp. 204–5).

Do We Know What Causes Autism?

There is still considerable discussion as to the exact causes of autism. During the 1950s and 1960s there was considerable speculation that the behaviors of parents in some way contributed to the development of autism in the infant or child. The implications of this theory were that parents were in some way to blame for the autism, and that the child should be given intensive psychotherapy to break through the "autistic barrier." These theories, and the therapies that came from them, were a double insult to parents. Not only were the parents in effect being blamed for their child's condition, but they were then subjected to often expensive therapies to "cure" the autism. There was no data to support the theory that parents caused autism, and the therapies provided were virtually useless in helping people with autism (see the review by Marian DeMyer, 1985, of theories about autism). Parents and families should be wary of any professional who tries to blame autism on styles of parenting, or promotes a single therapy to break through and cure the autism. These professional attitudes reflect a dangerously outdated view of autism, and place more burdens on already overburdened families (Sullivan, 1987).

The consensus among researchers now is that autism is the result of an injury or dysfunction to the central nervous system (Anderson and Hoshino, 1987; DeMyer, 1985). It seems that this injury could be the result of a wide variety of factors (Golden, 1987) including prenatal events (for example, toxemia, rubella), perinatal events (for example, trauma, anoxia), congenital factors (for example, microcephaly, tuberous sclerosis), metabolic factors (for example, PKU, Addison's disease), chromosomal factors (Fragile X Syndrome, XYY Syndrome), and other factors (for example, meningitis, encephalitis). Even with the evidence that autism is the result of a central nervous system injury, there is still no clear understanding of how these injuries lead to autistic behavior and characteristics, although there are some interesting possibilities for future research (Anderson and Hoshino, 1987, pp. 183–84; Ornitz, 1987, pp. 159–61). In other words, there seems to be no one cause for autism.

How Is Autism Different from Mental Retardation?

There are many similarities between autism and mental retardation. Like autism, mental retardation is both a behavioral syndrome and a developmental disability. Mental retardation is a more common disability than autism. As noted in a previous question, over 70 percent of persons with autism are also mentally retarded.

. Still, there are some differences between autism and mental retardation. A minority of the people with autism have normal or above normal intellectual abilities, and it would be counterproductive to try and serve these people in a program designed for people with mental retardation. Even when people with autism and mental retardation and those with mental retardation alone have similar levels of cognitive functioning there may be differences between the groups. The difference in symbolic play skills of autistic and severely mentally retarded children has been noted in a previous question (Wing et al., 1985), and there appear to be some differences between autistic and nonautistic children with mental retardation in the development of social skills (Sigman, Ungerer, Mundy, and Sherman, 1987, p. 114).

It would also be a mistake to make too much of the differences between these syndromes. Generally, people diagnosed as both autistic and mentally retarded respond well to techniques and programs that are effective for the mentally retarded population (Mesibov, Schopler, and Caison, 1989, p. 40). Of course, one of the characteristics of an effective program is the ability to adjust to account for individual needs, differences, and circumstances.

Is Autism a Type of Mental Illness?

This is another topic in autism that has been the source of considerable dispute in the past. Some researchers argued that autism was a type of schizophrenia, and that childhood schizophrenia and autism were essentially the same syndrome (Wing and Attwood, 1987, p. 14). Most researchers and professionals in the field of autism now accept that autism is not a mental illness, and is a syndrome clearly distinct from schizophrenia and other mental illnesses.

There are a number of differences between autism and

mental illness. The onset of autism is early, usually before the age of five, while the onset of most mental illnesses tends to be later into childhood or adolescence. People with autism are usually also mentally retarded, but mental illness is usually not associated with mental retardation. In most cases autism does not appear to be genetically based, but there is some evidence for the genetic basis of schizophrenia and some other mental illnesses. People with severe mental illness (especially schizophrenia) often experience delusions and hallucinations, while people with autism usually do not. In most cases of severe mental illness there are periods of remission and close to normal functioning, while people with autism do not usually fluctuate in this manner. Individuals with severe forms of such mental illness as obsessive-compulsive disorders are locked into rituals and schedules as much as any autistic person, but the person with the obsessive-compulsive disorder frequently struggles against the disorder, or tries to conceal it, while the person with autism usually shows no evidence of struggle or concealment (Wing and Attwood, 1987, pp. 15–16).

Once again, there are some similarities between autism and severe mental illness. The extreme social withdrawal and emotional flattening that is characteristic of severe schizophrenia may appear autistic. Since both autism and mental illness both occur along spectrums it can be difficult for even experienced clinicians and researchers to distinguish mental illness from autism in some cases. To further complicate the picture, in a small number of cases, it is possible that a person may be autistic and mentally ill, or even autistic, mentally ill, and mentally retarded (see Wing and Attwood, 1987, for a more complete discussion). In these cases, specialized services may be needed from both the mental retardation/developmental disabilities and the mental health service systems.

Most people with autism will benefit from the services and programs provided by the mental retardation/developmental disabilities service system, while people with mental illness receive services through the mental health service system. There are cases where certain individuals need services from both systems. In other cases, a person with autism will have an intelligence quotient (IQ) in the normal or above-normal range, and because of this, will not be eligible for services through developmental disabilities programs, but will need to apply for services through the mental health system.

What Is Kanner's Autism?

Kanner's Autism refers to the minority of people with autism (about 25–30 percent of the autistic population) who are not mentally retarded. People with Kanner's Autism have near-normal, normal, or even above-normal IQ scores, may be educated to the college or graduate level, and may often live independently in the community. Even though individuals with Kanner's Autism may have good vocabularies and excellent verbal skills in certain situations, these people still have many of the difficulties associated with the syndrome of autism. There are usually problems with common social skills and understanding the ordinary give-and-take of social interaction. Children and adults with Kanner's Autism also may have problems in the use and understanding of language, especially language associated with emotion or social relationships, although they may have very sophisticated vocabularies. Other problems may include a need for ritualistic behavior and a desire for extreme sameness in the environment.

In some ways, people with Kanner's Autism may be the least-served group of the autistic population. The person with Kanner's is usually aware that he or she is very different from other people, but may not know why. Educational and other programs that are needed and appropriate for people with autism and mental retardation are not the best type of program for people with Kanner's

Autism. Generally, the person with this diagnosis would not be eligible for services through the state developmental disabilities agencies, and may have to receive services through the mental health system. Unfortunately, there seems to be a greater chance of a person with Kanner's Autism "falling between the cracks" of the human service system than for a person with autism and mental retardation. See Kilman and Negri-Shoultz (1987) for a good discussion of programs for people with Kanner's Autism.

Is There Any Cure for Autism?

Studies of the natural history of autism (Paul, 1987) clearly show that the overwhelming majority of children who are properly diagnosed as autistic grow up to be adults with autism.

It must be understood that although there is no cure for autism, there is still a great deal that can be done for people with autism. There is good evidence that autistic people benefit from appropriate education and training, and with the proper support services, can live productive and happy lives in the community (see Sullivan, 1987). People with autism are individuals and so we cannot give a list of programs or services that would be appropriate for everyone with autism. There are, however, certain programs that are helpful for most children and adults with the diagnosis of autism. These programs as listed by the Autism Society of North Carolina (1989) include:

(1) Preschool programs for young children, and a properly structured and designed educational program;
(2) Recreational and other after-school and summer programs;
(3) Respite, parent training, appropriate counseling, and support for those families with an autistic family member who need these services;

(4) Residences in the local community for adults and for those children who cannot be maintained at home;

(5) Job training and preparation programs for teenagers and adults with autism, as well as programs such as supported employment for adults;

(6) Access to necessary medical, dental, and other services in the local community where possible;

(7) Any other service or support that will help a person with autism live as independently as possible in his/her local community.

While it would be irresponsible for any professional to lead a family to expect a cure for autism, the search for a cure may be part of the family's individual coping style (for example, Dreier, 1989), especially in times of stress. It may be an appropriate professional role to support the family as much as possible during the search for the "cure," while at the same time encouraging family members to look at other ways of coping with autism. It is important to maintain the attitude that people with autism can be helped to live fulfilling and productive lives in spite of their disabilities, and to give the family the opportunity to share this attitude.

Ultimately, the most important need of people with autism is to be accepted and understood as individuals. This understanding can be provided by anyone with the desire and patience to get involved; you do not need any special training, education, or expertise to provide this type of understanding. The willingness of one person simply to be a friend to a child or adult with autism, the acceptance of a person with autism in a social group, in a recreational activity, at the local supermarket, or at work, does as much to help as all the special programs and education. The special services are necessary for most people with autism, but these services in themselves are not sufficient in helping people with autism lead happy and productive lives. The role of ordinary people as friends, fellow workers, guides, supporters, and in countless other roles, is crucial to the success of any program for people with autism. With enough money you can buy experts, expertise, and training, but this will not mean anything for the person with autism unless he/she can be part of a community that cares for and accepts him/her.

Further Information

There are numerous books, journals, and articles available on every aspect of autism. The books listed below are comprehensive references, written by experts in autism.

Autism: A Reappraisal of Concepts and Treatment. Michael Rutter and Eric Shopler, editors. New York: Plenum Publishing, 1976.
Handbook of Autism and Pervasive Developmental Disorders. Donald Cohen and Anne Donnellan, editors. New York: John Wiley, 1987.

A number of organizations are concerned with the needs of children and adults with autism and their families. Membership of the organizations listed below consists of both families with a relative with autism as well as professionals and others providing services to people with autism. Both organizations have regular publications and frequent conferences. Readers who are interested either professionally or personally in autism should consider joining one or both organizations.

(1) Autism Society of America (ASA)*
Suite 1017
1234 Massachusetts Ave., NW
Washington, DC 20005

*Previously known as the National Society for Children and Adults with Autism.

ASA has a number of local chapters in various states and cities. The local chapter can be an important source of information and support for both families and professionals. For information on membership and local chapters, contact the Washington office of ASA.

(2) The Association for Persons with Severe Handicaps (TASH)
7010 Roosevelt Way, NE
Seattle, WA 98115

TASH is also an association of parents and professionals, but the focus of the organization is severe handicaps in general, including autism and mental retardation. Like ASA, TASH has local chapters in a number of states and regions.

(3) The Institute for Child Behavior Research is not strictly a membership organization, but it does publish an interesting and informative newsletter, *Autism Research Review International*. The institute was founded by Bernard Rimland, Ph.D., a pioneer in the field of autism research. The *Autism Review* newsletter reviews research on autism from around the world, and often includes lively discussions on many of the controversial issues in autism. To subscribe to the newsletter write to:

Institute for Child Behavior Research
4182 Adams Ave.
San Diego, CA 92116.

2

The Autism Wars:
A Brief History of a
Controversial Diagnosis

In 1938 Leo Kanner, a psychiatrist, reviewed information on eleven children who had been referred to him for treatment. Kanner concluded that these children "whose condition differs so markedly and uniquely from anything reported so far" (Kanner, 1985a, p. 11) suffered from the syndrome that he called infantile autism. Kanner was the first to classify many of the characteristics of the syndrome of autism, including the deficit in social relationships, problems in the use of language, repetitive behaviors, unusual reactions to environmental stimuli, etc. As Michael Rutter (1985, p. 51) observed, Kanner's stature as a clinical observer has increased over the years because his initial descriptions of children with autism were so clear and accurate. Rutter also recommended that anyone who wanted to know what children with autism were like should read Kanner's paper, first published in 1943: I think this is an excellent recommendation, few modern clinical studies match Kanner for the clarity of his description and his obvious concern for the people he was describing.

Kanner assumed that autism was caused by some unknown biological factor. However, he noted that the parents of many of the children he studied were not very "warmhearted," and that "even some of the happiest marriages are rather cold and formal affairs" (1985a, p. 50). Although Kanner's 1943 paper generated little immediate response, by 1950 professional interest in the syndrome of autism was beginning to increase in the United States, the United Kingdom, and Western Europe (Donnellan, 1985).

Many therapists, especially those interested in psychoanalytic theory, became very interested in the possibility that the child with autism was basically intelligent but had withdrawn from social contact due to traumatic events in the environment, specifically the lack of warmth from one or both parents. In 1959, Bruno Bettelheim, a prominent psychologist, published an article "Joey, a 'Mechanical Boy'" in *Scientific American*. This article, with its description of a child with autism and implication that underneath the strange and withdrawn behavior was a very intelligent boy, caught the imagination of both professionals and public (Donnellan, 1985, pp. 3–4). The implications of this view of autism were that parents in some way contributed to the development of the severe withdrawal of the person with autism, and that children with autism should be treated with intensive psychotherapy in order to bring them out of their shell of withdrawal.

It would be wrong to assume that all professionals in the 1950s who wrote about autism approached the topic in the same way as Bettelheim. In her excellent review of the research on autism in the 1950s and 1960s Marian DeMyer (1985, pp. 261–62) identified the three basic theories concerning the cause of autism during that period. These theories were that the parents caused autism with their cold, rejecting behavior; or that the child with autism was suffering from some biologically based condition that was not the result of parent behavior; or that an already vulnerable child with biological condition had that condition made worse by the behavior of the parents. The best-known, and probably the most dogmatic, proponent of the view that autism is the result of parental behavior is Bruno Bettelheim. In his book *The Empty Fortress* (1967) Bettelheim argued that the most effective technique for working with children with autism was to remove the child from the family and then provide the child with intensive psychoanalytic treatment. Bettelheim provided no evidence to support his theories about autism, and there is no evidence that the type of treatment he recommended is useful in working with most children or adults with autism (Riddle, 1987, pp. 535–36).

The 1960s were a time of ferment and significant change in the field of autism. First, a number of psychoanalysts were expressing doubts as to whether individual psychotherapy was the best way to provide services to the majority of the autistic population (Riddle, 1987, pp. 534–35). Second, Ferster (1985) in an influential paper first published in 1961, argued that many of the behaviors, including language, of children with autism could be changed and improved with a systematic program of behavior modification. Ferster also made the interesting observation that even the most bizarre behaviors of people with autism may be a form of communication, and the person exhibiting these behaviors may be trained to communicate the same message in a more appropriate manner (LaVigna, 1985). Ferster's paper released a flood of behavior modification research and practice in the field of autism. Eventually, the various forms of behavior modification theory were to take over from psychoanalysis as the dominant theory underlying educational and other programs for people with autism. Third, during the early 1960s, efforts began to develop a reliable and valid method of diagnosing autism. Obviously, without a consistent system of diagnosis, it is impossible to do much useful research on autism in general or the particular needs of children and adults with autism. While progress was made during the 1960s and 1970s on diagnosis, there is still some controversy about this issue. Fourth, a psychologist, who also happened to be the parent of a child with autism, wrote a short book published in 1964.

The parent, Bernard Rimland, and his book, *Infantile Autism* (1964), were to be two of the most important factors in research on autism during the decade. The book is relatively brief, but was written with an underlying current of outrage and anger toward those professionals who would blame parents for the development of autism in a child. Rimland dissected much of the previous theorizing about autism, and found it to consist in many cases of a lot of armchair speculation based on knowledge of relatively few actual cases of autism. He clearly listed the evidence that autism was due to biological causes that had nothing to do with the child-rearing practices of the parents. Although Rimland's book was initially rejected by many professionals, the evidence he cited was confirmed by subsequent research.

Parents responded to Rimland's book with a mixture of rage and relief. Frank Warren (1978, p. 196) gave a strong but not unusual parental response: "An abject apology is called for by all that horde of ignorant physicians, smug psychiatrists, know-it-all social workers, inept educators, claptrap therapists." Warren went on to indicate how important professionals who truly understood the syndrome of autism were to families.

Some of Bettelheim's views are still held by a small number of professionals in the US, and many psychoanalysts in Western Europe also seem to share his views of autism (Everard, 1987, p. 744). In spite of this, I think Anne Donnellan (1985, p. 5) was correct when she wrote: "Rimland laid to rest the ghost of psychogenesis (i.e., the theory that parental behavior causes autism) so persuasively that no serious behavioral scientist has raised it again."

Bernard Rimland would be an important figure in the history of autism on the basis of his book alone. During the 1960s Rimland went on to found the organization that is now known as the Autism Society of America (ASA). Membership of ASA consisted of parents and professionals who rejected the theory of the psychogenesis of autism. ASA continues to advocate for services for persons with autism and their families.

Some parents, such as Amy Lettick at Benhaven, went on to found their own schools when the public schools refused to educate their children with autism. A group of parents in North Carolina, along with Eric Schopler and Robert Reichler of the University of North Carolina, persuaded the state legislature to fund Division TEACCH (Treatment and Education of Autistic and related Communication handicapped Children), a statewide program providing services to children and adults with autism and their families (Warren, 1987). Division TEACCH now offers training and consultation not only in North Carolina but in other states and foreign countries. There are many other examples, continuing up to the present, of parents and sympathetic professionals collaborating in order to develop or obtain services for children and adults with autism.

In the late 1960s and early 1970s researchers and clinicians like Schopler and Reichler (1971), and Ivar Lovaas (Lovaas, Koegel, Simmons, and Long, 1973), argued that not only were parents not responsible for causing autism, but that treatment and education programs for children and adults with autism required the active cooperation of parents in order to be effective.

With the passage of the Education of All Handicapped Children Act in 1975, there was a national requirement that children with handicaps be educated, and education should take place in local schools where possible. This act also required that families be given the opportunity to participate in the development of an educational program for a child with handicaps. This law made a tremendous difference in expanding the opportunities for children with autism to receive an education and become as independent as possible. Options for adults with autism in the areas of community residences and job training and support have expanded greatly over the past twenty years. In spite of these achievements, there is no room for complacency. Children with autism still miss out on the education that they are entitled to by law in many circumstances. Programs for adults in many areas of the country may be insufficient, or nonexistent in some regions.

The 1970s were a time of exciting developments in special education and other programs for children and adults with autism. Behavior modification programs for young children with autism provided evidence that the children, with intensive training and support, could improve language and other skills, and that this improvement could be maintained over a period of years in the right program (see for example, Lovaas, Koegel, Simmons, and Long, 1973). There was a better understanding of the crucial role of the family in programs for both children and adults with autism, as well as recognition that parents were often the experts when it came to the needs and best interests of their handicapped child. Research on special education in the 1970s and 1980s certainly did not answer all the questions about effective educational techniques in autism, but began to provide classroom teachers with some practical information on how to teach both children and adults with autism. Research on various medications, and vitamin and diet therapies created excitement in the field, although at times there was too much excitement as certain drug, vitamin, or diet therapies were proclaimed as "cures" for autism. There is no medication, diet, or vitamin therapy that will cure autism, but there are interesting possibilities, especially in the area of medication, which have formed the basis for some effective treatments in association with the proper educational or behavioral program.

In spite of these important developments in the 1970s, which have continued into this decade, the lives of many people with autism remained fairly grim. The majority of adults with autism in the US during the 1970s lived in large institutions. Kanner (1985b) followed up on the eleven children he studied in 1943 in a report published twenty-eight years later. He found that some of the original children were able to function at jobs in the local community and were doing well. In contrast, those who as adults were living in large state institutions frequently withdrew from all social contact and experienced "a total retreat to near-nothingness" (p. 223). At the end of his report, Kanner was realistic but somewhat pessimistic over the progress he saw in the field of autism: "This thirty-year follow-up has not indicated too much concrete progress from the time of the original report, beyond the refinement of diagnostic criteria. There has been a hodge-podge of theories, hypotheses, and speculations, and there have been many valiant, well-motivated attempts at alleviation awaiting eventual evaluation" (Kanner, 1985b, p. 234).

Still, the foundations for a better life for children and adults with autism were laid during the 1970s. Changes in federal and state policies, often driven by lawsuits, encouraged the movement of people from the large institutions to smaller community residences. One of the many little-known heroes of this movement was an eccentric, dynamic former jazz musician turned psychologist named Marc Gold. Gold had an almost passionate interest in the abilities and needs of people with severe handicaps, including those with mental retardation and autism. In a series of fascinating research reports Gold and others (Wehman, 1988) demonstrated that adults with some of the most severe handicaps, including individuals who were deaf, blind, and mentally retarded, could be trained to perform valuable tasks including the complex assembly of electronic components and products such as chain saws.

From these small beginnings in the 1970s a whole series of programs known as supported employment gave people with even the severest handicaps the chance to work in the community for wages along with nonhandicapped people. Supported employment for people with autism has been successful in many areas of the US, and is giving thousands of adults with autism the chance to live and work in their local communities (McCarthy, Fender, and Fender, 1988).

The work of Kanner, Gold, and others who are still relatively unknown did not solve all the problems faced by people with autism, but their greatness lies in their ability to see that there are no "throwaway" or "useless" people, but that people with the severest handicaps are individuals who all have much to contribute to our society.

Continuing Controversies

Autism is still a mystery in spite of the progress in research and services. Although there is now a general understanding that autism is a biologically based condition, there are disputes as to the use of certain behavior modification techniques and medications, whether all children with autism should be educated in regular schools and classrooms or if separate educational programs are ever justified, which type of residential program is the most appropriate for children and adults with autism. At times these disputes have been as heated as the previous disagreements about the causes of autism. In some cases, professional journals and meetings have been closed to the opinions of those who disagree with the prevailing wisdom.

I think those of us in the field of autism who are often caught up in disagreements and controversies need to learn some of the lessons of the history of the syndrome. The first lesson is that dogmatism about most issues in autism is not appropriate. We still know relatively little about the syndrome and the best way to help people with autism. Second, even when people are "wrong" they may have something to teach us. Although I have painted a fairly negative picture of many of the early psychoanalysts who tried to work with children with autism, this picture is unfair in some ways. While the dogmatism of many of the early writings is irritating, the authors of the papers were genuinely trying to understand autism and to help people with autism. The psychoanalytic psychotherapy was not helpful for most people with autism, but as Riddle (1987) pointed out, these authors at least accepted that people with autism could be helped, and in some way laid the groundwork for later progress in the field. As I noted previously, many of these early authors also admitted that their procedures were not effective with many children with autism. Even if we only learn to have the courage to admit the truth when we are wrong, and when we don't know—the kind of courage a number of the psychoanalytic authors had—then the history lesson will not be in vain. Anne Donnellan observed that "very little about autism is ever noncontroversial" (1985, p. 5). This observation is likely to be accurate for a long time into the future.

Further Information

The best single source of information on the brief history of autism is *Classic Readings in Autism,* edited by Anne M. Donnellan (1985, New York: Teacher's College Press). The book contains reprints of many of the classic writings about autism, along with commentaries.

Bernard Rimland's *Infantile Autism* is still worth reading. The book is clear, concise, and devastating in its attack on many of the psychoanalytic theories about autism.

3

A Free, Appropriate Public Education

Other days we celebrate the everyday miracles: support from those who love us, teachers who are amazingly caring and understanding.

> —From "Rain Boy" by Patricia A. Dreier, in the *New York Times* (Feb. 19, 1989).

We cannot teach her anything. She has never been in school, although she was on the waiting list for the school for low-grade children for four years. Her family reports that when she lived at home an elderly woman from the neighborhood was able to teach her to sing and brush her hair.

> —Case report, nearly fifty years old, on a woman with severe mental retardation and autism. The woman now (1989) lives happily in a small group home.

The school just sent him home and said they couldn't handle him and they would not take him back. We've had him home for over a year, and the school district hasn't done anything. I didn't think they could treat kids this way.

> —Parent of teenage boy with autism (1988).

In 1975, as noted, the United States Congress passed the Education for All Handicapped Children Act, otherwise known as Public Law (PL) 94–142. This legislation mandated that all handicapped children from age three to age twenty-one are entitled to a "free, appropriate, public education." More recent legislation (Public Law 99–457) has extended the right to special education to infants, toddlers, and preschool children with handicaps, although special education programs for very young children will vary from state to state. Parents, counselors, and others who are interested in special education services can usually obtain information from their local school district or an office of their state department of education.

Public Law 94–142 required that handicapped children in need of special education have an educational program designed to meet their specific individual needs; that the educational program be in the "least restrictive environment," that is, as much as possible in the child's home community; that parents have the opportunity to participate in the development of the educational program for their child; and that each child in special education have an appropriate individualized education plan (IEP).

While the mandates of PL 94–142 have given thousands of children with handicaps the chance to receive a good education, and to become independent and productive citizens, there are still situations where children with autism and other handicaps simply do not receive the educational services guaranteed by law. In the past year I have been involved in a number of cases from a variety of states in which children with autism were sent home from school and left at home with their families with virtually no educational or other services. These periods at home were not for short periods of time: in one case an adolescent boy was at home for over a year. The lesson is that families, counselors, teachers, and all those who care about people with autism cannot afford to be complacent about programs and services, even if the programs are required by law.

How Does a Child Receive Special Education Services?

If a parent, legal guardian, or foster parent has a child who needs special education, the process for requesting services is fairly standard throughout the United States. The procedures described below will apply to school-age children (those who are five or older): special education services for infants, toddlers, and preschool children may be provided by the local school district, the state health department, or some other agency. Even if the local school district does not provide special education for preschool children, the district staff is usually able to refer parents to the appropriate agency. If the district is unable to help, the head office of the state department of education (usually located in your state's capital city) can probably help. Another way of obtaining quick and accurate information about preschool services is through the office of the state governor, or of your local state representative or senator. In dealing with staff of a number of state politicians in a variety of states, I always found the staff members sympathetic, courteous, and able to obtain the necessary information quickly and efficiently. Do not forget the local chapters of such organizations as the Autism Society of America and TASH discussed in chapter 1: the people in these chapters know local services well and are often parents who have been through the process.

Parents with a school-age child should request an assessment of their child from their local school district in writing, if they feel their child needs special education. Generally, the school district must respond with a date for an assessment within a certain period of time, usually thirty days after the receipt of the written request. The office of the principal of the local school, or the office of the district superintendent, should be able to tell parents where to direct their requests for an assessment. This assessment must be multidisciplinary, that is, the assessment must be done by a team of professionals, usually including a teacher, psychologist, social worker, speech therapist. Sometimes, depending on the needs of the referred child, the team may also consist of a nurse, physician, occupational or physical therapist, or other professional. The team must first answer two basic questions. First, is the referred child handicapped? Second, does this handicap require some type of special education, equipment, or service for the child to make educational progress? Some parents and counselors, in my experience, are confused about these requirements. It is not simply enough to state that a child has a certain handicapping conditions, there must also be a demonstration that because of the handicap, the child is in need of special education. For most children with severe handicapping condition there is usually no dispute about the need for special education. Where handicaps are less obvious, there sometimes may be a reasonable disagreement as to the need for special education.

Once the multidisciplinary team has completed its report, a copy of the report is forwarded to the parents, and the team usually meets with the parents to discuss the results of the evaluation. This is the time that disagreements about the need for special education are likely to surface. If the parents disagree with the conclusions of the multidisciplinary team they have the option of appealing: the appeals process should be explained during the meeting. It is important for parents and counselors to understand fully the appeals process. This process can be full of traps for the unwary and the uninformed, with very specific requirements that appeals be in writing or that the appeal be registered within a certain period of time. State departments of education, and most local school districts, have books explaining appeals that are usually available free to any interested person.

Even if the appeals are not successful, there is the option of taking legal action against the school district in order to obtain the necessary special education and other services. Congress recently passed the Handicapped Children's Protection Act of 1986 (Public Law 99–372) which provides that parents and legal guardians who win legal or administrative hearings when trying to obtain services under Public Law 94–142 may be reimbursed for attorney and other expenses (Florian and West, 1989). Even with this new law, there are a number of important factors to keep in mind. First, as any attorney will admit, there is no guarantee that the plaintiffs will win even if they have a good case. Second, legal proceedings are usually lengthy and very expensive. Third, to have a reasonable chance of success the parents will need an attorney who is experienced and knowledgeable in the area of special education and disability law. Such attorneys are difficult to find, especially outside the major metropolitan areas, and when they are found they are usually swamped with cases. The best sources of information about these attorneys is the local chapter of the Autism Society of America, TASH, or similar organizations: the referral sources of the local bar association or the law school of a university may also be helpful. Fourth, Public Law 99–372 emphasizes that parents and school districts should make reasonable compromises. If a school district offers a settlement that the parents reject, and the district settlement is found to be reasonable by the court, the parents would not be reimbursed for attorney's fees (Florian and West, 1989, p. 6). Fifth, even if you "win" you may not win much. I have seen a number of unfortunate cases where parents won the right to an appropriate special education for their child, only to find that there is no appropriate program near them, or that appropriate programs may not have the capacity to accept the child even though funding is available. The moral is that compromise and collaboration with school districts is usually the best strategy, although parents need to be informed of their rights to administrative or legal appeals as a last resort. Actually, less than 1 percent of the parents involved in the special education system have needed to resort to legal action to obtain their rights (Florian and West, 1989, p. 7). I hope this means that conflicts between parents and school districts are frequently resolved in a constructive manner. A less optimistic interpretation may be that parents are not aware of their right to appeal decisions concerning special education.

The Individualized Education Plan (IEP)

When a child is found in need of special education, an educational program is developed based on the child's specific needs. This program is known as the IEP. The IEP is a written plan that outlines the educational goals and objectives the child will be working on for the coming year; the IEP also lists other services (such as Occupational or Physical Therapy) if needed, and how often these services will be provided.

The federal and state regulations have requirements for the development of a valid IEP. The IEP must be developed within thirty days after the multidisciplinary team has determined that a child needs special education. The IEP itself must follow certain guidelines (Rosenberg, 1987, p. 619). First, the IEP must contain a clear description of the child's current level of educational performance. Second, there must be a list of annual goals and short-term instructional objectives. The annual goals are a statement of where the child's educational performance will be one year from the present if the educational program is effective: the instructional objectives are the "stepping stones" to the annual goal, that is, those skills that must be mastered before the annual goal can be attained. Instructional objectives are generally reviewed quarterly. Third, there must be a list of the specific educational and other services the child will receive in the coming year in order to attain the annual goals. Fourth, information must be included as to the extent to which the child will participate in regular education with nonhandicapped children. While Public Law 94–142 does not mandate that handicapped children be educated with nonhandicapped children, there is the expectation that the handicapped children will be involved in regular educational activities as much as possible. Fifth, the IEP must include objective procedures and criteria, such as gains on a standardized or teacher-made test or changes in the frequency or intensity of behavior, so that progress toward the annual goals can be observed. This last requirement often causes counselors not used to dealing with special education some problems. In order to participate formally as part of a student's educational team, the counselor must specify in advance the expected outcomes of counseling or therapy: these outcomes must be in observable or measurable terms. This issue will be discussed further in the section on the counselor as member of the educational team later in this chapter.

The IEP is developed at a planning meeting that the child's parents, teacher, the supervisor of special education for the school, and other members of the staff attend. An IEP is not implemented until the parents have given their written consent to the educational program. If the parents do not agree with the services or program outlined in the IEP, they have the option of appealing through the school district appeals process. They also have the option of taking legal action once they have exhausted the district appeals process. While parents need to know their rights of appeal, it is obviously in the best interests of all concerned if disagreements can be ironed out constructively at the IEP meeting.

Parents have the right to bring outside experts or other staff with them to the IEP meeting to evaluate the educational program proposed by the school district. Other parents prefer to bring a friend, relative, or neighbor for moral support to the meeting. In my experience, some of the most valuable and penetrating questions at IEP meetings have been asked by parents or their friends or neighbors who have no professional knowledge of special education. At one meeting a teacher was describing a complex educational program to teach a severely handicapped eighteen-year-old student to identify colors. The program was creative, well designed, and the teacher was enthusiastic: most of the members of the IEP team (including me) thought it would be an excellent program. Then a friend of the student's mother, a woman who had known the student since he was a baby, asked, "Can he zip up his pants after going to the toilet yet?" The answer was no. The neighbor said nothing further but her point was clear; color identification was wonderful, but let's put more time and effort into the basics. The purpose of the IEP team meeting is to prioritize those educational needs that are most relevant to the student. All students in special education have a huge list of potential needs; the question becomes one of which needs are most important to the student now, and which skills will help that student to be as independent as possible in the future. These questions can really only be answered effectively if the student's parents are at the IEP meeting.

Roles for Counselors and Other Concerned People

Counselors and others who are concerned about a child with autism and his/her family can play a number of vital roles in the special education process. The roles described below are not mutually exclusive, so that a counselor may find him/herself playing two or more roles at once. I think it is important to have some awareness of the role that is called for at a particular time, and whether the counselor has the skills or desire to play that role. Obviously, open and honest communication with the family as to which role the counselor can and cannot play is essential.

(1) Family friend

This is not a professional role at all, but someone who is concerned about the family and is willing to do anything possible to help out. This role may call for a person to go with a family member to the IEP or other meetings to provide moral support: the friend may say nothing during the meeting but his/her presence has provided more support than hours of professional counseling. A friend may offer to help by taking a child with autism out for a walk, or to the park or zoo, in order to give the family a short break. The friend may help involve a child with autism in a local play group, or Boy Scout or Girl Scout troop, or church or social group, or even help find a job after school or during the summer for a teenager with autism. It is virtually impossible to describe all the helpful things that a friend can do: sometimes it is doing nothing more than listening without trying to offer quick solutions or pat answers that only serve to make us feel better.

Family friend is one of the most powerful and satisfying roles that any person can take on, and requires no professional training or degree.

(2) Supportive family counseling

Family counseling will be discussed at greater length in another chapter. A counselor with some knowledge of autism and of the special education system can give families a chance to explore their feelings and frustrations and clarify the options available to them. Counselors need to be aware that families with an autistic child or adult living with them may have a history of bad experiences with human service professionals. If the family has not experienced this personally, many families are well informed and are aware of the history of some professionals blaming parents for the development of the child's autism.

The counselor needs to demonstrate a realistic understanding of the syndrome of autism, and also to have some idea of the resources that may be available to the family in the local community. As families go through the inevitable ups and downs of their child's educational progress, and experience the frustrations of dealing with special education and other programs, I believe it can be helpful for them to discuss their feelings and frustrations with a counselor. Some families find long-term counseling helpful, while others may wish for short-term counseling to help them deal with a specific situation. The most successful counseling I have seen has been short-term individual counseling followed by the parent's participating in a support group with other parents. It is important to remember that parents and families are individual in their needs and situations. Not all families with children or adults with autism want or need supportive counseling.

A trap for the unwary counselor is what I call the "brush-off" referral. Sometimes, when parents and school districts or other agencies are in conflict on a specific issue, or number of issues, the parents are referred for counseling. This can be a way for the agency to avoid dealing with the conflict in a constructive manner. Obviously, the counseling is unlikely to be successful in this situation. If a counselor is faced with what appears to be this type of referral he/she must clarify the goals of the counseling from the beginning, and come to an understanding with the parent as to whether they really want counseling. A way of dealing with the situation is to discuss the source of conflict that precipitated the referral and to help the family become aware of the options available to them as well as possible ways of resolving the conflict.

(3) Member of the educational team

It is possible to include counseling on the IEP as a service related to helping the student attain his/her annual goals. There are a number of opportunities for the counselor in this role. The counselor could provide counseling either individually or in a group to students with autism. Or the counselor could provide counseling to families or groups of families concerning the educational programs designed for their children. The difference between this role and the supportive family counseling role described above is that the primary focus of the counselor as a member of the educational team is the attainment of the student's annual goals. This still leaves room for a wide variety of counseling interventions. But the counselor as a member of the educational team needs to have objective, measurable outcomes for services provided.

Counselors who are employed in special education settings, or those counselors who use behavior modification techniques as part of their usual practice, generally have no problem with the requirement for measurable outcomes of therapy. Even if a counselor is not familiar with special education or behavior modification, this need for specific outcomes of therapy need not be an insurmountable obstacle. There is evidence (Fischer, 1978, pp. 79–80) that effective counseling usually requires the counselor to negotiate specific outcomes in the beginning of the counseling relationship. There are good references available for developing measurable outcomes for individual (for example, Fischer, 1978) or group (for example, Rose, 1977) counseling.

Individual counseling with children or adults with autism has generally been unsuccessful in the past. But I think there is a role for appropriate individual counseling with some persons with autism. The counseling should be very concrete and focused on recent events and the development of certain social or work skills. Helpful counseling approaches may include general social skills training (Kilman and Negri-Shoultz, 1987), William Glasser's Reality Therapy (1975), or the use of techniques such as behavioral contracting (for example, DeRisi and Butz, 1975) as the basis for counseling with individuals or groups. These techniques would also be appropriate for small group counseling with appropriate students with autism. In some cases, a small group approach may be more effective than individual counseling, especially in training various social skills.

Of the total population of students with autism, only a relatively small proportion will have the cognitive or language abilities to benefit from individual counseling, and even in this small number of cases it is not realistic to expect that counseling will lead to dramatic changes in the student's behavior. As an adjunct to a comprehensive program of special education or vocational training and support, counseling may be an important part of an appropriate educational program for some children or adults with autism.

Some interesting research in training young children with autism in various social skills has emphasized the importance of the opportunity for these children to participate in the ordinary life of the community. In some cases, nonhandicapped children of the same chronological age as the children with autism have been effective trainers of social skills in group settings. There are activities, programs, and games that a group leader can use to train students with autism in a variety of important skills (see Donnellan and Neel, 1986; Gaylord-Ross, Stremel-Campbell, and Storey, 1986).

Parent training, either individually or in groups, is also a good way for a counselor to participate as a member of the educational team. Parent training requires considerable sensitivity, knowledge, and understanding on the part of the counselor. Not all parents need, want, or have time for parent training. In some cases, the parents will know much more about a particular topic than the counselor. This should not be a problem for a counselor secure in his/her professional skills and identity and willing to learn from the group setting. At times, the best thing the counselor can do is to get the group going and then get out of the way as the parents provide support and information for each other. Rose (1977) has a good discussion of parent support and training groups, as well as ways of developing measurable outcomes for these groups. Parent training can be tricky for professionals who may find the parents being "trained" know more about some topics than the professional. There is a further discussion of this issue later in this chapter.

The role of member of the educational team calls for more professional knowledge of autism and of the special education system than do the other roles discussed previously. Counselors who wish to become members of the educational team can usually learn the necessary information in a relatively short period of time if they have the willingness to listen and want to make the effort to learn. Much of the actual learning will result from listening to people with autism and their families. Good counselors in autism, like good counselors in all fields, will not be afraid to say, "I don't know," will develop people and literature as sources of further information, and will know when they are out of their depth and it is time to call in someone else.

(4) Family advocate

This role also calls for the counselor to have some fairly intensive knowledge of the field of autism, and especially of the requirements of special education and other relevant service systems. It is the advocate's task not only to provide emotional and moral support, but also to marshal information and resources to assist a family to obtain the services they need. Advocates usually know not only the structure of local organizations and service systems, but also have a wide network of personal contacts in many different organizations. The advocate must not only know the theoretical rights of people with autism but also how most effectively to go about obtaining these rights. Good advocates know that there are costs as well as benefits of pursuing legal and administrative appeals, and the importance of cooperating as much as possible with local agencies in order to obtain the necessary services.

Advocates learn the lesson that all politicians learn at one time or another: "Never promise nor threaten what you can't deliver." Ineffective advocates rely heavily on threats and emotional outbursts at meetings in order to attain their goals. Good advocates, like good attorneys, know how important it is to be civil and polite even in the middle of the most heated disagreements.

Sometimes it is the advocate's role to provide technical assistance to those who are supposed to be the experts. A number of parents and other advocates have told me stories of being asked to design educational programs for a child with autism when the advocate has complained about the inadequacy of the current program. While advocates should be as cooperative as possible in providing information and support, it should be clear that it is not the advocate's job to provide an appropriate special education for a student with autism.

The best advocates are the members of the immediate family of the person with autism. Although advocates from outside the family can be helpful, in certain circumstances only a family member can make a phone call or write a letter that is likely to have any effect. Especially in contacting members of school boards, or federal or state legislators, members of the family are the only really effective advocates. Counselors who act as advocates are generally better off remaining in the background and providing moral support and information where necessary.

It is not necessary for a good advocate to have a degree in special education, but the advocate should have some understanding of the basic components of an effective educational program for people with autism. Some important questions about programs for both children and adults with autism include:

(a) Is there a curriculum?

Any educational program needs some kind of guiding philosophy, an outline of the important areas for instruction, and a concept of how the instruction is to be organized. Any program for people with autism that does not have, or use, a proper curriculum is likely to be disorganized and fragmented (Scott and Gilliam, 1987).

The curriculum should give appropriate emphasis to the development of social and language/communication skills, and have a focus on those skills that the person with autism will need to function as independently as possible. A curriculum in a program for adolescents and adults with autism should emphasize the development of work and independent living skills.

There are a number of good resources that could be used to develop an appropriate curriculum, for example, Johnson and Koegel (1982), Mirenda and Donnellan (1987), and Simonson (1979).

(b) Do members of the staff have instructional control?

Instructional control refers to those skills that a student needs before he/she is able to learn. For example, if a student is constantly running around a classroom, or frequently engaging in repetitive body motions, it is unlikely that the student will pay attention in a learning situation. Developing instructional control such as looking at a teacher giving an instruction, staying in one place for a period of time, following direction from the teacher, etc., is one of the most frustrating and aggravating tasks for any special education teacher. Yet without these basic skills it is unlikely that the student will learn anything useful. I have seen a number of classrooms where the teacher does not have the information, ability, or willingness to develop a good program of instructional control.

An important aspect of instructional control, and of the education of children and adults with autism in general, is the requirement for structure. Structure refers to stability and predictability not only in actual teaching and in the daily routines of the program, but also serious consideration in setting up the physical environment in order to help the student learn and reduce distractions. Structure does not mean rigid, inflexible routines or procedures, but a flexibility according to the needs of individual students within a general framework. The basis for structure in an educational program for children and adults with autism is a curriculum that is comprehensive enough to address the goals of the program, and is clear enough to focus on the educational priorities of the program. Structure depends on a trained and motivated teaching staff and managers and supervisors who support and hold staff accountable for the development of an appropriate structure. There is no doubt that some kind of appropriate structure is needed for an effective educational program for students with autism (Olley, 1987). There are a number of teaching techniques and practices that are effective with students with autism and other severe handicaps (see Schopler and Reichler, 1979, and Mesibov, Schopler, Schaffer, and Landrus, 1988, for good examples) but all these techniques require a clear, consistent, and structured approach to teaching.

Some good references in the area of instructional control include Koegel, Rincover, and Russo (1982), and Lutzker, Campbell, Newman, and Harrold (1989) for a discussion of compliance training in the home.

(c) Do staff members understand autism?
Because autism is a relatively rare syndrome, children with autism are sometimes placed in classrooms with children with mental retardation or other syndromes. This may work well for some students; for other students the whole situation becomes a disaster. The student with autism is obviously very different from the other students, and the teacher becomes frustrated because many of the usual teaching techniques do not seem to work. There are many

good references in the area of teaching techniques but teachers are unlikely to learn these techniques from a book. In this case either the student should be transferred to another more appropriate special education program, or a consultant should be brought into the classroom to recommend and demonstrate the appropriate techniques for the staff. Donnellan (1987) described a comprehensive training program for teachers and other professionals interested in working in the field of autism. Most state departments of education and many of the larger school districts have consultants available to provide training and information for teachers and other involved in the education of children with autism. Nationally known programs such as Division TEACCH in North Carolina offer teacher training seminars in many aspects of autism during the summer. Usually, a local university department of special education can provide information on training opportunities, and may have experts of their own available for consultation.

(d) Does the staff have a good understanding of behavior modification, and use it appropriately?

There is little doubt now that effective educational programs for people with autism make use of many of the techniques of behavior modification. Essential components of this approach in autism include a full evaluation of the student's needs that will include an evaluation of the communicative intent of behavior: some apparently meaningless behaviors may be an attempt by the student to communicate a desire or need, and this is crucial information in designing a behavioral or educational program. Other components of a good behavioral program include clear descriptions of the behaviors to be changed (either increased or decreased), as well as a reliable system for collecting data on the effectiveness of the behavioral program. Changes in the program should be the result of frequent reevaluations of the data on student progress, or lack of progress. The book by Ian Evans and Luanna Meyer (1985) is a practical overview of behavior modification for students with autism and other severe handicaps, and is an excellent reference for classroom teachers, parents, and advocates.

(e) Does the staff expect students to learn?
This is so basic that many of us forget about this expectation entirely. Unfortunately, especially in programs for students with severe handicaps, teachers, parents, and others may have very low expectations for the students. A delicate balancing act is frequently required. While it certainly would not be helpful to have expectations so high that they could never be fulfilled, it is my experience that it is more common to have expectations of students that are too low. The research in special education is very clear: effective teachers have clear expectations that their students will learn, set educational goals and objectives that the student can master, keep data on student educational achievement, and use a variety of alternative techniques when the student is not keeping pace with the material (Bickel and Bickel, 1986, and Zigmond and Miller, 1986, have good discussions of effective educational assessment and instructional techniques in special education).

A teacher's expectation that a student with autism can learn is not only a positive factor in the classroom. I have seen families gain hope where previously they had only despair when a teacher or other staff member had clear, realistic expectations that a child or adult with autism could learn and grow. Jane Schulz (1978, p. 35), parent of a handicapped young adult and a professional special educator, remembered the effect of a good teacher on her and her son: "My son had one teacher who expected him to learn. She respected him; she valued him as a person who was capable of learning and accepting responsibility. She valued me as a parent but let me know she had everything under control in the classroom." Even a brief contact with a good teacher can make a real difference in a family's life. I remember a few years ago when parents brought their five-year-old daughter with mental retardation and autism to a program for an educational evaluation. The family was from a very small, rural school district and the little girl had been labeled as "unteachable." The family had experienced so much rejection in the past that the fear and exhaustion were almost etched in their faces. I was trying, with little success, to put the parents at ease, when a teacher came into my office to ask a question. The teacher looked at the little girl, broke into a wide smile, and said, "You're so pretty, I wish I had you in my class." A sense of relief broke over the office like a wave. Both parents beamed proudly as the little girl left the office to take a walk with the teacher.

(f) Are parents considered part of the educational team? Even though parent participation in educational planning is required by Public Law 94–142, there are very good reasons to include parents on the IEP team even if there were no legislative requirement. Parents are usually the experts on the needs of their own child, and have a lot of valuable information and opinions to contribute to the development of a good educational program. At times, the parent's technical knowledge is at least equal to, and may be superior to, the knowledge of the professionals on the team. I have been to IEP meetings where the parents have clearly explained to professionals the need for certain behavioral and educational techniques. On a number of occasions professionals tried to "educate" parents about handicaps only to be seriously embarrassed when the parents knew as much, or more, than the professional. Jane Schulz (1978, p. 33) knows the pitfalls of underestimating parents: "The current concept of parent training is extremely insulting. Some of my colleagues told me of an encounter with a young mother and her two boys, aged seven and twelve, both mentally retarded and blind. My associate suggested that parent training was indicated. I wondered at the time who we knew who could tell this mother anything. In fact, I immediately wanted to meet and learn from a woman who had raised children with such complicated problems.

This is not to suggest that parents know everything or that professionals have no role in services to people with handicaps or that parent training is never appropriate. The vast majority of parents know they need the knowledge and expertise of a wide variety of professionals. There is evidence that appropriate parent training is helpful both to parents and to children with autism and other developmental disabilities (Marcus, Lansing, Andrews, and Schopler, 1978). The need for a clear recognition of the importance of parental opinions and knowledge is crucial. An advocate can play an extremely constructive role in supporting parents during the IEP process and helping to resolve the inevitable disagreements and disputes in a constructive manner.

Perhaps the most delicate responsibility of the advocate is helping the family balance the costs and benefits of a certain course of action. In many parts of the country parents may not have a variety of programs to choose if one program is not meeting their child's needs. This is especially true of services for adults with autism. In almost all areas, services for adults may not be sufficient to meet the needs of all those who need the service. Parents may feel grateful for any service provided, and might not feel comfortable complaining about the quality of the service. It is the advocate's responsibility to be aware of these realities and know how the family feels about their situation. In some cases, one option for parents is to get together with others and try to create their own programs. While this is not a solution for everyone, some of the most creative and vital agencies providing services today for people with autism began as an attempt by a parent or group of parents to meet the needs of a child or adult who had been rejected by all the local schools and agencies.

An appropriate education is the foundation of a life of independence and dignity for most people with autism. A proper education is not only crucial to the individual with autism, but can also be an important factor in helping families survive and cope. In too many cases the development of an educational program is left to the professionals in the fields of special education and behavior modification. While the skills and techniques of the special educator and the behaviorist are important, parents too have information and opinions that can determine the success or failure of an educational program for a child or adult with autism. A counselor, member of the clergy, family friend, or neighbor, with an open mind and a willingness to listen, can support a family through the educational process, or be part of a successful educational program for a person with autism by including that person in some of the everyday activities of the local community.

Further Information

There are many books and articles on educational programs for children and adults with autism. The interested reader will find many sources of information in the references to this chapter. For information on educational programs for children with autism in a particular area, the special education department of the local school district is probably the best place to start. Information on programs for adults with autism may be more difficult to obtain, and it is possible there might not be any local programs available. The best places to obtain information on programs for adults would probably be through the local office of the state agency responsible for mental retardation and other developmental disabilities: other potential sources of information include the Autism Society of America, a local branch of the Association for Retarded Citizens (ARC), or possibly, the local office of the United Way or similar organization.

Parents may have to enlist the help of school-board members, or of state representatives or senators, in order to bring political pressure on agencies or school districts. Contacting politicians can frequently (but not always) be an effective strategy: see Warren (1987) for good advice in this area. At times it may be necessary to bring a lawsuit to obtain an appropriate education for a child with autism. Lawsuits have been effective, but a lot of thought needs to go into the potential benefits and risks of a suit. Contrary to what parents may hear from some advocates, the parent does not always win! It is possible for a parent to lose a suit and be saddled with large legal costs. A good attorney with knowledge and experience of disability law and the legal system is essential. Referrals for good attorneys in this area may possibly be obtained from the local chapters of the Autism Society of America or other advocacy groups, a family attorney, or the law school of a local university. All states have offices of Protection and Advocacy (often known as P & A) who are responsible for advocating for and protecting people with handicaps. The P & A office usually employs attorneys, but they are often swamped with cases. However, the P & A office may be able to give a referral to a good private attorney. P & A has different names in different states, but the local office of your state representative or senator should be able to give you the telephone number. Another good source of information on services is the local United Way. In some states there are private agencies that have a P & A function.

Parents and professionals who are interested in training in specific educational techniques appropriate for children and adults with autism could contact the special education department of a local university or college. Division TEACCH in North Carolina frequently offers training seminars, as well as consultation and technical assistance services, which may be helpful for anyone involved in the field of autism. For further information on Division TEACCH programs contact:

Dr. Eric Schopler, Director
Division TEACCH
CB# 7180, Medical School Wing E, UNC-CH
Chapel Hill, NC 27599-7180.

4

Working with Families

Living with an autistic child is an exhilarating and hum-
bling experience, an emotional roller coaster without an
end—or a seat belt. Michael is frustrating, puzzling, tiring,
loving, trusting, and sometimes hilarious. It's like seeing
a body turned inside out—a soul exposed. He exposes the
souls of others, too.

> —From "Rain Boy" by Patricia A. Dreier,
> in the *New York Times* (Feb. 19, 1989).

It has become very prevalent in special education departments of colleges and universities to offer courses on working with parents. I cringe at the thought of some of the
course syllabi I have reviewed. In many of these courses,
very limited attention is directed toward helping parents
solve the day-to-day problems that almost invariably are
encountered, yet weeks are devoted to the psychological
insight approach to parental guilt.

> —Ann Turnbull (1978, p. 138), parent and special
> education professional.

Parents are beginning to be dealt with from the point of
view of mutuality. . . . They have of late been included
in the therapeutic efforts, not as etiological culprits, nor
merely as recipients of drug prescriptions and of thou-shalt
and thou-shalt-not rules, but as actively contributing co-
therapists.

> —Leo Kanner (1985, p. 234: originally published in 1971).

Autism is such a mystery. Half the time I don't know what
is the right thing to do.
                    —Parent of a young child with autism.

It is now generally accepted that parents of children with autism are in no way responsible for their child's
autism (see Plienis, Robbins, and Dunlap, 1988, pp. 32–33,
for a concise review of the evidence). But there is also
evidence that parents of a child with autism are faced
with many stresses, including possible emotional and marital conflicts, problems in dealing with their child's behaviors, anxiety about the future, social isolation, and
financial and other difficulties (Wolf, Noh, Fisman, and
Speechley, 1989). The stress on families with a child or
adult with autism is apparently greater than stress generally experienced by families with children with other
handicaps: families with more severely handicapped children or adults seem to have more stress than those with
a less severely handicapped family member (Plienis et al.,
1988, pp. 33–34; Wolf et al., 1989, pp. 157–58).

Professional counselors and other people in the community can give valuable support to families with a child
or adult with autism. because autism is in many ways such
a mysterious and complex condition, it is not surprising
that families usually need support in many different areas
of life and in a variety of situations. While every family
and family situation is different, I believe there are important general guidelines to be considered by counselors
and others who want to help families.

Suggestions for Those Who Want to Help

(1) Know your own feelings and values

Knowing yourself is an important foundation for any effective counseling relationship. If a counselor does not

genuinely believe that all people with autism, no matter how handicapped, have value as individual human beings, and can learn and grow and become more independent, then it is unlikely that counselor can provide effective help to the family. Parents and counselors usually bring their own values to the relationship, and problems arise when these sometimes unacknowledged values conflict. A counselor should be aware of how his or her values have been formed by a society that, according to some surveys (Yuker, 1988) does not have a very positive view of persons with severe disabilities. Value conflicts may not necessarily mean the end of the counseling relationship with the family. If the counselor and the family agree on the fundamental value of the worth of every person, no matter how handicapped, then it may be possible to "agree to disagree" about certain values and work on other issues. The resolution of this conflict may not be successful if the counselor does not have the awareness to clarify his or her own values and seek to clarify the values of the members of the family (which may differ from one family member to another as well).

This emphasis on positive values does not mean that the counselor ignores the less positive aspects of the autistic child or adult's personality. People with autism are individuals and some are more likable than others, just like nonhandicapped people. The counselor can expect to feel joy and satisfaction, as well as frustration, anger, and anxiety as in any counseling relationship. The counselor can always choose to end his or her involvement with autism: this is not an option for the family.

Another possible source of value conflict is the counselor who is firmly convinced of the value of the child or adult with autism, but may have trouble accepting the needs and value of the other members of the family. There are professionals and others who rapidly become indignant with any real or imagined insult to people with handicaps, but who then can be scathingly critical of nonhandicapped people including parents. The complete focus on the needs of the child or adult with autism, to the exclusion of the needs of the family, is not really in the interests of anyone. People with handicaps and their families need each other. The realities of life also mean that not every issue, conflict, or difficulty in a family where there is a family member with autism is necessarily related to the handicap. At times, families are referred to counselors or other professionals who specialize in the field of autism, and who may see every problem or difficulty as related to that issue. I have to remind myself frequently to really listen to what the members of the family are saying, and to take the time to view the whole family system, before assuming that the problem is related to autism.

I do not assume that value conflicts or differences are always the fault of the counselor or someone trying to help the family. Some families with a child or adult with autism living with them may consult a counselor or seek help in times of great stress or anxiety. The members of the family may be anxious, depressed, socially isolated, angry, or resentful, perhaps with ambivalent feelings toward professionals (Roos, 1978). The counselor must be strong enough in his or her professional and personal identity to be able to work through these strong feelings in a positive way with the members of the family. Counselors and others who are not secure enough to deal with anger and resentment in a constructive manner may find themselves resenting the "ingratitude" of some of the families. I am not arguing that all parents of children or adults with autism are constantly angry or bitter, neither are all families saints or martyrs. Members of families are ordinary people coping the best way they can with stresses of a difficult and sometimes impossible nature. A counselor who is aware of his or her own weaknesses and human failings will not expect perfection from others.

Counselors need a realistic understanding of their own needs and limitations. Sometimes in our need to be helpful we promise too much. All of us in the human service field have probably, at one time or another, fallen into the trap of trying to be the "rescuer." This fantasy is especially dangerous when dealing with the syndrome of autism. Any counselor or other professional who believes that he or she can bring a person "out of autism," or can meet all the needs of a family, seriously misunderstands the nature of autism.

There is no magic involved in working with a person with autism or his or her family. The most effective people in the field of autism are those who are aware of their own needs, feelings, and limitations, willing to learn and make mistakes, have a genuine respect for all persons with autism and their families, and enjoy what they are doing. I remember the advice of a parent of an adult with autism when speaking to staff who work in programs for people with autism: "If you really hate what you're doing, do everyone, including yourself, a favor, and do something else." This is certainly the best advice for people working in the field of autism I ever heard.

(2) Remember that families differ from each other

There is no program, technique, medication, or type of counseling that is appropriate for all persons with autism or for their families. Just as individuals with autism need an educational and behavioral program designed for their specific needs if it is to be effective, so there is no one service or program that is appropriate for all families. It is essential that the counselor or other person in a helping situation with a family take the time to get to know the unique family situation, and to clarify the needs and expectations of all the family members, before beginning any kind of service.

(3) Remember that families are systems

Although systems theory has been the foundation for many of the theories of family therapy for over twenty years, I know I often forget how complex and interrelated even a small family can be. One of the basic tenets of family therapy based on systems theory is that a change in one part of the system (one family member) will lead to changes in other parts of the system (other members) or may even change the system completely. A behavior modification program that successfully changes the behavior of a child with autism at home may have unexpected effects on other family members: these effects may be good or bad depending on the circumstances and situation. Family-support programs that allow parents to participate in training their child in some important skill find that success at this task often helps the parent cope with feelings of depression and hopelessness about the future of their child (Marcus and Schopler, 1987). On the other hand, a family-intervention program that requires that one or both parents spend a considerable amount of time with the child with autism could lead to marital difficulties or to resentment or unhappiness from the nonhandicapped children in the family. Obviously, it is not possible to look ahead and see every possible consequence of everything you do with a family, but it helps to have as full an evaluation as possible of the family's current situation, opinions, and needs when you first start working with the family. Benson and Turnbull (1986, pp. 150–51) developed a useful guideline for assessing the needs of a family from a systems perspective. It also helps to expect that unexpected changes are likely as the result of services provided to the family.

In cases where the family is poor, or has problems in the areas of substance or alcohol abuse, it is even more important to take a systems perspective of the family situation. Generally, poor families with children with autism and other handicaps are not well served by most family support programs (Strain and Odom, 1986, pp. 64–66). These families may have immediate needs in the areas of financial support, employment, food, or housing that must be met before any counseling, parent training, or other services can be delivered. Even middle-class or relatively affluent parents of a child with autism may be so distracted by the child's need for training in basic living skills such as eating, dressing, or toileting that they may not be interested in any form of counseling relationship. Naturally the family's priorities and preferences need to be respected in this situation. Successful programs for families in poverty or with many complex needs such as the one developed by Lutzker et al. (1989), have to provide an array of services according to the priorities of the individual family. Lutzker's program involved not only behavior modification programs for the child but also marital counseling, referrals to substance abuse and other agencies, information on financial assistance and credit counseling, assisting parents in finding employment, educating families about child development, and helping to correct safety hazards in the family home.

No individual counselor could, or should try to, provide all the services described above. Counselors should be willing to spend time exploring the broad family system and the family's own goals and priorities, before trying to provide services. In many cases there will be "nitty-gritty" issues that need to be resolved in some way before an effective counseling relationship can be established. A good counselor will be aware of the services that exist in the local community and be able to make referrals when necessary.

Viewing the family as a system makes life for the counselor much more complicated. There is a lot of skill, developed with training, experience, and making mistakes, needed to look at the family as a system and to see which parts of the system may be relevant in a given circumstance and situation. Even with the skill and experience there are always surprises; that is what makes it so frustrating, and so interesting.

(4) Remember that family needs change over time

Families face different needs and challenges over the life cycle of the family member with autism. Parents of an infant or preschool child may have a strong feeling that their child is different from other children, but may not be able to obtain a clear diagnosis of their child's problem from any professional. The parents may be uneasy and frustrated with the reassurances from professionals and others that "everything is fine." If a diagnosis of autism is made, there may also be false reassurances that the child will recover, or at the opposite extreme, the recommendation that the family place the child in an institution. Even worse, the family could be faced with a number of conflicting diagnoses from different professionals with different theoretical perspectives. Some families spend considerable time and money going from one professional to another trying to obtain a clear diagnosis and explanation of their child's condition. Unfortunately, they are not likely to hear the words, "I don't know." Families in this situation may be accused of "doctor shopping," or be piously told, "Labels don't mean anything." But labels do mean something! A clear and appropriate diagnosis is a guide to services needed now and in the future, and will be required for the child to receive appropriate educational and other services. Donnellan and Mirenda (1984, pp. 18–19) noted that this search for a clear diagnosis is sometimes misinterpreted as a grief reaction by the parents to the diagnosis of a handicap. When parents are faced with a confusing and frustrating environment when they are trying to get help for their child it is not surprising that some respond with anger, frustration, and grief. Counselors should avoid the temptation to see deep psychological causes in what are normal reactions to a number of very clear environmental stresses. It is important to understand the very practical need for the family to have a clear diagnosis of their child's condition.

If there is a diagnosis of autism, some parents may respond with grief, anxiety, and depression. At this time, the family may embark on a search for a "cure" for autism. As noted in the first chapter, this search for a cure is not necessarily pathological, but may be a stage of adjustment to the diagnosis of autism for a particular family. Of course, there is always the danger that the search becomes counterproductive as the family becomes more disappointed, socially isolated, and financially drained as one "cure" after another fails to materialize.

The challenges faced by a family will change as the family member with autism gets older, goes through adolescence, and faces the demands of the adult world. This will be discussed in a later chapter. The main point is that those in a helping relationship with the family should understand that family needs change over time. Families with a preschool child with autism, and those with an adult family member with autism, may be similar in some ways but will generally be facing different situations and will often need different types of services.

(5) Families have strengths as well as needs

With all the emphasis on the problems faced by families it is very easy to get the impression that families with a child or adult with autism at home are so beset by emotional conflicts and various demands that they are virtually helpless. This is far from the truth. Virtually all families have many strengths and coping skills, and manage the demands of their environments surprisingly well. Many of the families I have been in contact with over the years deeply resent what seems to be the preoccupation of some professionals with the problems of families with handicapped children. A number of surveys of parents of children with severe handicaps have found that, while there may be problems, the majority of the families have a very positive view of the contribution of the child with the handicap to the family life in general (Summers, Behr, and Turnbull, 1989). Programs for families with young children with handicaps that focus on family strengths (for example, Dunst, Trivette, Gordon, and Pletcher, 1989) have been quite successful.

This is not an argument that families have no problems. But it seems logical for those who wish to help build on the family strengths and adaptations that already exist in order to help deal with any problems. Any type of program, service, or assistance to a family that is based on the assumption that the family is a helpless recipient of services with no resources of its own may possibly make the family situation worse rather than better (see Dunst et al., 1989, and Summers et al., 1989 for an excellent discussion of this issue).

(6) Remember that fathers are different from mothers

This seems so obvious that it is not worth discussing. Unfortunately, much of the research on families with children with handicaps has relied almost entirely on mothers for information (Bristol and Gallagher, 1986, pp. 82–83). Those studies that included fathers (for example, Wolf et al., 1989) found differences between fathers and mothers in their reactions to the stress of caring for a handicapped child. These possible differences should not be exaggerated, and individual situations will vary, but it would be important to make an effort to include fathers in discussing and planning services or help for the family. Counselors should remember that fathers and mothers may have different perceptions of family situations and needs.

(7) Remember the brothers and sisters

If the child with autism has brothers and sisters, they may have contributions and skills, as well as needs and desires, which need to be considered when providing help or support to the family. There is not much research on the siblings of children with handicaps, but the research available suggests that brothers and sisters generally respond positively to their handicapped sibling (Simeonsson and Bailey, 1986). In some cases, brothers and sisters have been trained as tutors and trainers for the child with handicaps (Simeonsson and Bailey, 1986). There are also situations where the brother or sister may resent the amount of parental attention devoted to the handicapped child. In their review of the research, Simeonsson and Bailey (1986, p. 74) found that brothers and sisters who are either younger or closer in age to the child with handicaps seemed to have the most difficulty adjusting, while older siblings seemed to adjust fairly well.

A family may seek the services of a counselor for a nonhandicapped brother or sister because of problems of adjusting to the demands placed on the family by the child with autism. The nonhandicapped child may benefit from the attention of a sympathetic adult who can listen in a nonjudgmental way to the child's perception of the family situation. In one case of successful family counseling I remember, the parents received supportive marital counseling and information on resources for their child, a successful home behavior modification program was developed for the child with handicaps, and a nonhandicapped sister who resented the attention paid the handicapped child was given special attention by a graduate student who was a trainee in the family support agency. This combination of services was very successful. Not all situations are resolved so well, but I doubt that the parental counseling or the behavior modification program would have been as successful in this family without

special consideration for the needs of the nonhandicapped sister. A counselor or any other person may provide a valuable service for a family with a child with autism
by simply including the child's nonhandicapped brothers
or sisters in social, sporting, or recreational events, or even
by giving them some extra attention at times.

Counselors may consider developing a support group
for the brothers and sisters of children with autism. The
counselor should be familiar with the syndrome of autism
and aware that not all siblings want or need to be involved
in such groups. The type of group experience will depend
on the ages and needs of the siblings involved. I feel that
the most effective types of sibling groups combine practical information about the handicap, a chance for the
siblings to share experiences, feelings, and information
with others, as well as suggestions for handling any feelings of resentment, anger, guilt, or embarrassment that
may come from having a brother or sister with autism.
Naturally, the information presented, and the activities
in the group, should be appropriate to the ages and developmental level of the siblings in the group. Siblings
of very different ages should probably not be in one
group, but it might be helpful to have a teenage sibling
help as assistant leader of the group or activity leader
for younger children. There is some good information
on the needs of siblings of children with autism (Sullivan,
1979) and on sibling groups (Hamlin and Timberlake,
1981). Support groups for adult siblings of individuals
with autism may also be an appropriate service for some
families.

(8) Remember the importance of social support

Social support is the assistance, emotional and practical,
provided by friends, relatives, neighbors, and other good
people. We know that families of persons with autism are
often more socially isolated than other families in the com-

munity. Research also suggests (Wolf et al., 1989) that the depression and feelings of hopelessness felt by some parents (especially mothers) of children with autism can be reduced where social support is available. Unfortunately, at times professional services for families with handicapped children have resulted in the family's becoming more isolated and dependent on professional services (Dunst et al., 1989). This dependence is not necessarily positive; professionals can resign, or be transferred, or become more interested in something else, and agencies can change or discontinue services because of budget cuts or staff shortages.

Parents who feel the need for more social support might be put in contact with other parents of children or adults with autism or other disabilities, and be encouraged to support each other informally as needed: the counselor would only intervene at the request of the families. This mutual support network of families, sometimes known as a parent-to-parent network, has been a good source of support for many families. As noted previously, a number of successful intervention programs with families (Dunst et al., 1989; Strain and Odom, 1986, p. 66) rely heavily on the families' delivering services to each other, with backup professional services when needed or requested.

Other families with children with handicaps are not the only sources of support available. The counselor may assist families who wish to become more involved in social activities, or groups in the local community may make the initial contact with these groups. There will be times when the counselor may be asked to provide family counseling so that parents may develop a better relationship with their own parents or brothers and sisters in order to broaden the family's network of social support. There is a growing interest in researching the importance of social support to families with a child or adult with autism. I also expect to see in the future more family-support programs that are guided and directed by families and more programs in which professionals provide the necessary backup services.

(9) Remember the importance of faith for some families

Phillip Roos (1978, p. 25), a psychologist and parent of a young woman with mental retardation, noted that it was sometimes difficult for parents to have professionals listen to their search for meaning and faith as a way of coping with a child with handicaps. Some, but certainly not all, parents find meaning for their situation in various religious beliefs. It seems to me that a number of counselors and other human service professionals are uncomfortable with expressions of faith or religious belief, and may tend to see this faith as an unhealthy denial of the realities of the situation.

In my experience religious faith is generally a very positive force in the lives of many families. The faith usually affirms the humanity and dignity of the person with the handicap, and gives a framework of hope and understanding especially during times of heavy stress. If the family is affiliated with a local church or temple this may also be a valuable source of social support. Members of the clergy are now frequently trained as pastoral counselors, and for families with a strong religious background a referral for pastoral counseling would be appropriate.

Families with strong beliefs may still have their periods of doubt, frustration, and anger. Religious organizations that speak forcefully on the rights of people with handicaps may not be so welcoming when a person with autism or a family member actually shows up at the local church. Still, I believe that religious faith is an important, and greatly underestimated, factor in helping many families cope with the demands and stresses of living with a person with autism.

(10) Do not be too quick to offer reassurance or make promises

Many parents told me of their anger and frustration at certain professionals and others in the helping role who offer reassurance before they even hear about the problem. In many cases, this reassurance comes from a brief newspaper article, a discussion on a television or radio talk show, or some similar source. One mother was discussing her problems caring for her adolescent daughter with autism with a therapist at a local community mental health center. The therapist said abruptly, "Oh, autism. They can do a lot for that now. I saw it in the paper last week." The article in the newspaper was a brief description of a trial of a new medication with *four* children with autism: only two of the children improved as a result of the medication. Later trials of the medication did not show even this modest level of success. This need to offer false reassurance is not confined to those professionals who know nothing about autism. I was at a presentation by an expert in the field of behavior modification who had considerable experience in the field of autism. An obviously distraught mother stood up to describe her situation of living with her son, a young man with autism who was extremely aggressive toward the other members of the family and who also engaged in self-injurious behavior. Before the mother could finish her statement a member of the panel on the stage said that there were "all kinds of good programs to treat those behaviors." The expert nodded in agreement. After the presentation, I approached the members of the panel and asked for information on all those "good programs." The main presenter and the panelist who offered the reassurance glared at me for a moment. They both then rattled off a series of names of researchers and journal articles about behavior modification programs for the treatment of aggression and self-injury. I was familiar with most of the names and articles and I knew the treatment programs were carried out in hospital or residential settings with twenty-four-hour staffing. I asked for programs that were implemented in the home by the family since this seemed to be the situation of the woman asking the question. There was a brief, frosty silence. The panelist said he was sure there were programs like that, but that he had to rush to catch a plane.

I am not using these incidents to give professionals a bad name, or as an attempt to display my own superior clinical skills and insight. I have also fallen into the trap of making quick promises or reassurances as a response to my own feelings of inadequacy or helplessness. Somehow it feels good just to say reassuring things even if you don't really believe them. But these reassurances ring false almost as soon as they leave your lips, and they can stop an effective helping relationship with the family at the very beginning.

Dealing with Conflict and Disagreements

Some kinds of conflicts and disagreements are inevitable in almost any relationship. When a family is dealing with such a complex phenomenon as the syndrome of autism, there is a greater chance for misunderstanding between family members and the professional or other person trying to help.

Any person with experience in the human services, or of life in general, is well aware there are no magic solutions to conflict situations. Some conflicts and disagreements may not be resolvable. But in my experience most disagreements can be resolved, or simply mutually tolerated, while the helping relationship develops. There are a few basic steps listed below that may be helpful in dealing with a conflict situation.

(1) What is the conflict about?

This may sound like a very simple question, and in some cases it is. In other cases the issue or situation that becomes the focus of the immediate disagreement is not the basic issue at all. Is there a conflict of basic values? Are there unstated expectations at work on the part of the counselor and the family or both? Is there conflict among the members of the family as well as with the counselor? Is it a difference in personal style? There is an almost endless list of possible causes of conflict, depending on the specific situation. In my experience there are three basic sources of conflict in a relationship with a family. The first is a disagreement about basic values that are important in the working relationship. The second is simply a personal dislike for the counselor or for the family. The third is the presence of unstated expectations in the relationship. Unstated expectations could involve something as basic as being punctual for meetings, or the expectation by the counselor that the family should drop everything to discuss their situation, or the expectation by the family that the counselor will always be available for meetings or telephone conversations.

Clarification of the reason or reasons at the root of the conflict or disagreement can be a difficult, painful process for all involved. Yet there will be no progress toward resolving or dealing with the disagreement until these basic issues are identified; the process of identification requires that everyone involved risk being open and honest with each other.

(2) Can the conflict be resolved?

There are conflicts, disagreements, or even personal dislikes so basic or so intense that they may not be able to be resolved in a reasonable time, if at all. The counselor and the family may decide that the time and energy needed to resolve the conflict would be better spent on other issues, and the family might seek help from another source, or the counselor may make a referral to another professional.

Fortunately this type of conflict is rare. The presence of this intense conflict does not imply that there is a serious problem with the family, or that the counselor is incompetent or insensitive.

(3) Can we agree to disagree?

In everyday life we all go through our work and personal lives not dealing with issues with certain people because the issue creates so much conflict. While this may be counterproductive at times when issues have to be resolved, it is not a bad way to handle many of the conflicts in relationships with families. Everyone in the relationship consciously avoids dealing with a certain issue while working together fairly successfully on other issues. It is my experience that this approach is only successful after the basic source of conflict has been identified, and when all involved make a conscious effort to agree to disagree and work on other things.

(4) Is a compromise possible?

Many disagreements get so tangled up in emotions and ego that the possibility of a reasonable compromise is never explored. Daily life continues only because we all make reasonable compromises at one time or another. I have been surprised at how many heated conflicts can be resolved with honesty, good faith, and some effort from those involved. Whether a compromise is possible will depend on the issue and the people involved, and before any compromise will work the basis for the disagreement must be clarified.

(5) Let the family make the final decision

This is not an argument that families are always right: families make mistakes, but then so do professionals. Once the family has the information it needs to make an informed decision, it is the family's right and responsibility to make that decision. The professional's involvement with autism can always end as a result of a change of jobs, career, or assignment: the family's involvement is permanent. For this reason, it is essential that the family be supported in their right to make decisions, and have the best possible information on the possible consequences of these decisions.

In very rare and serious cases, the decision-making power of the family concerning a child or adult with autism may be legally taken away and a legal guardian appointed. But this is the rare exception that proves the rule. Families usually have the ultimate responsibility for caring for a person with autism, often for life; given this responsibility, the family must have the freedom and the information to make the decisions they feel are best.

The "Good Parents" Syndrome

There has been a great and positive change over the past thirty years with the increased understanding and respect for the importance of families in the lives of children and adults with autism. A number of effective programs for parents and other family members have been developed including respite services, support groups for parents and siblings, behavioral and educational training for parents, supportive counseling, and many others. Some of the most effective programs have been provided in the home. Home-based behavior modification and education programs for children with autism, which also include supportive counseling and case-management services for the other members of the family where necessary, are known to be effective (Hemsley, Howlin, Berger, Hersov, Holbrook, Rutter, and Yule, 1978; Plienis, Robbins, and Dunlap, 1988; Schopler, 1978). In an interesting study of home-based behavioral training of families with children with autism, Koegel, Schriebman, Britten, Burke, and O'Neill (1982) found that 25 to 50 hours of behavioral training in the family home was more effective than 225 hours of behavioral treatment in a clinic, and that the families receiving home-based services reported increased leisure and recreation time over a group of families receiving similar treatment in a clinic setting.

Even though these programs and services have been of great assistance to many families, there are also dangers associated with them. I agree with a number of authors (for example, Strain and Odom, 1986; Benson and Turnbull, 1986) that there is a tendency in the professional community to see these effective services and then assume that "good parents" would want or need these services. This is what I call the "good parents syndrome." If support groups are provided, or behavior modification training, or respite care, or there is a need for political lobbying, then "good parents" will be willing to participate. There is nothing wrong with any of these services and good parents participate in them, and help fund and run many of them. But in our enthusiasm for certain types of services we cannot forget that families have individual needs and situations. Just as there are no programs and services that are good for every person with autism, there are no specific programs and services that are automatically good or necessary for every family.

Good programs for families such as Division TEACCH (Marcus and Schopler, 1987) in North Carolina and the APT Training Program in Boston (Cutler and Kozloff, 1987), recognize the importance of working with parents and other family members as collaborators, and the necessity for families to have the option of choosing services and programs according to their own unique needs and desires.

Further Information

For excellent discussions of the basic principles important to all programs and services for families, see Donnellan and Mirenda (1984) and Marcus and Schopler (1987). The reference section of this chapter also has a number of other useful discussions and descriptions of programs for families.

5

Working with Adolescents

We've had our problems, but it's nice to see her grow up
and be more independent.
                    —Parent of a teenage girl with autism.

I don't know what to do. When he was younger we could
control that behavior at home. Now he's a teenager, I'm
just scared he's going to hurt someone—sometimes I can't
even think of him as my son.
                    —Parent of a teenage boy with autism.

The adolescent years are tough for teenagers
and their parents. Adolescence is a time of change, uncer-
tainty, and frustration, but also of growth and the development of those skills needed to function as an adult. This
is especially true for teenagers with autism and their families. Some research (Marcus and Schopler, 1987, p. 508)
has indicated that the teenage years are the most stressful
time of all for parents and families of a child with autism.

A teenager with autism faces all the usual struggles and
hopes of adolescence, in addition to some special challenges and situations.

Issues Faced by Teenagers with Autism

(1) Physical growth and development

As teenagers with autism grow physically a number of issues become important for them and their families. If the teenager is one of the minority of individuals with autism who has severe problems with such behaviors as assault or self-injury, the situation at home may become intolerable for the whole family, and a residential setting outside of the home may be needed. Assault and self-injury are not the only behaviors that can create serious problems in the home. A teenager with autism who shows no fear or awareness of the potential dangers of heat, traffic, or electricity, or other dangerous situations, may not be able to remain safely in some homes. Other behaviors such as pica (eating nonfood items) may also pose serious danger to the adolescent with autism. These behaviors are not confined to teenagers and can obviously be a serious problem even with very young children. It seems in some cases that the behavior becomes worse during adolescence, or in other cases because the child becomes physically larger the difficulty in managing the behaviors in the home setting increases tremendously. Of course, not all teenagers with autism develop severe behavior problems, but when this occurs there can be a devastating effect on the whole family.

An important area of physical and emotional growth during adolescence is in the area of sexuality. The development of sexual feelings and desires is a natural part of growing up for people with autism as for anyone else. There may be times and situations where the teenager with autism does not have the necessary social or cognitive skills to express his/her sexuality appropriately. In some cases there may be instances of inappropriate touching of others, or of public masturbation. These situations are obviously very stressful for the teenager who may have little or no understanding as to why his/her behavior is so disturbing for others. Parents or siblings who have to try and control the public sexual behavior of the teenager are also under tremendous stress. There is also the well-founded concern that a teenager with autism may be sexually victimized by others. Sexuality is such a complex issue that numerous books have been devoted to the topic. Like so many other issues in autism there are no simple solutions or "quick fixes" to problems in the area of sexuality. The best approach seems to be ongoing programs of sex education that are appropriate to the level of cognitive development and the specific needs of the person with autism. If there are problems with certain sexual behaviors, a behavior modification program, along with appropriate sex education, may be needed. Melone and Lettick (1983) and Ford (1987) are good sources of information on sex education programs for adolescents with autism.

Teenagers with autism are at greater risk during the adolescent years for the development of seizures. This is unusual because the general population is at less risk for seizures during adolescence (Paul, 1987, p. 123). Parents and other family members should be aware that seizures are not necessarily only major convulsions, but can also be manifested by quite subtle changes in behavior. Once again, it is important to remember that not all teenagers with autism develop seizures; this discussion refers to a minority of the population. If a parent or relative is concerned about the possibility of seizure activity, a physician should be consulted for an evaluation or for referral to the appropriate neurologist.

(2) Need for independence

Most teenagers with autism, like their nonhandicapped counterparts, start feeling an increasing need for independence and autonomy during adolescence. This is an important step toward adult life, but can also be a source of conflict within the family. It is possible that the adolescent with autism may not be able to handle safely the responsibilities of greater autonomy in the same way as a nonhandicapped adolescent. At the same time, it is important for the teenager with autism to have some opportunity to become more independent and to explore options for the future. This may involve exposing him or her to a wider variety of leisure activities and encouraging him/her to choose from a number of preferred activities. The possibility of a job after school or on the weekends should also be explored. A job not only provides the opportunity to earn money, but also gives the worker the chance to explore possible future career choices. In addition, a job may provide the opportunity to become more integrated into the life of the local community, and give the person with autism the chance to make social contact with other nonhandicapped people.

(3) Being part of the group

One of the major characteristics of the syndrome of autism is severe difficulty in developing appropriate social relationships. For some people with autism this difficulty becomes obvious when the person resists most kinds of social contact and withdraws into solitary activities at every opportunity. Others appear very interested in social relationships, but seem to lack the basic skills to understand and maintain the give and take of everyday communication with others.

Even for those teenagers with autism who are intensely solitary, there often seems to be a realization that they are not part of the group of adolescents they see in their families and local communities. These teenagers see their brothers and sisters and other adolescents going out on dates, driving cars, working after school, and generally preparing for adult life. Where the person with autism is chronologically a teenager but is also mentally retarded and functions at the level of a three- or four-year-old, there may be additional problems. The teenager may be interested in the games and activities of young nonhandicapped children, and want to participate in these activities. When the teenager was younger this might not have been a problem, but parents of preschool nonhandicapped children are not likely to be comfortable with a teenager playing with their children, even if they have a good understanding of autism. During adolescence there is a chance that the relatively limited social contacts previously available to a solitary young child with autism may shrink even further. I believe that those persons with autism who are quite severely handicapped still may have a feeling that they are becoming more isolated, even though they may have no real understanding of the situation.

Probably the most effective way of dealing with increasing isolation and shrinking social contacts for a person with autism is the same way most nonhandicapped people would deal with the problem. The answer seems to be to try and make as many social contacts with other teenagers or adults in the community as possible. One way of making these contacts is through work. Another way is through participation in social, church, or even volunteer activities with others of a similar age group. This has to be done carefully and thoughtfully, respecting the individual needs and preferences of the person with autism. Perhaps very limited partial participation in a group or activity might be an appropriate goal. At the same time, the needs of the nonhandicapped people in the group need to be met in some way as well. If the teenager with autism is working, the employer should feel that he or she is receiving services that are worth the paycheck. In social groups, the emphasis should not only be on what the person with autism needs or wants, but also on how can that person contribute to the group? Once again, we are not talking about magic solutions. The community involvement is usually only successful with a lot of patience and understanding, and a willingness to try and fail many times. At the end of all this effort, the teenager with autism may be a peripheral member of a group, but if this group membership does something to meet both individual and group needs, then all the effort has been worth it.

It would be wrong to leave this discussion of autism and adolescence giving the impression that all teenagers with autism are in a constant state of turmoil and social isolation. While there are problems that cannot be ignored, the vast majority of teenagers with autism, like teenagers everywhere, manage to pass through adolescence to adulthood successfully.

Issues Faced by Families

Because the family is a system, the issues faced by a teenager with autism during adolescence also have an effect on all the other members of the family. All families and all teenagers are unique, so that not every family necessarily faces the issues discussed below. In my experience, however, many families with a child with autism will face at least some of these issues and problems at one time or another.

(1) Physical growth and development of the teenager with autism

Obviously, any medical or behavioral problems of the teenager with autism will affect the other members of the family. These problems are not only emotional and psychological problems. The family may be faced with severe financial burdens in trying to obtain the proper medical treatment, or educational or residential services for their child with autism. This is not a problem confined to the teenage years, but it seems the stresses of adolescence may make what was a fairly manageable situation at home into an intolerable situation for all family members. The majority of teenagers with autism do *not* have these severe behavior problems. Still, in my experience, one of the more common reasons given by parents and families seeking professional help is the need to cope with certain behavioral problems in the home.

At times, the family situation becomes so stressful that it is not in the best interests of the family or the child with autism for the child to remain in the home. Parents and family members who come to this decision usually do so after making almost superhuman efforts to keep the child or teenager with autism at home. Parents are often ambivalent about the decision to place a child or teenager in a residential program, and there may even be severe disagreements within the family about the decision. Sometimes, relatives or even neighbors who have no understanding of the family situation, and may not even know the child with autism, make unhelpful comments about the situation, which adds to the family stress. Because caring for a child at home is much less expensive than residential care, the school or other social service system might vigorously oppose the parental request for a residential program. School districts will pay for residential programs for children with autism only if the program is "educationally necessary" for the child and no appropriate special education program is available locally. Residential programs for children and teenagers can be very expensive, so the family will usually face intense opposition from school districts and other agencies. Many residential programs cost around a hundred thousand dollars annually, which means that the vast majority of parents could not possibly pay for residential services with their own resources. If funding is obtained from the school system or other agency, there is no guarantee that the residential program will have vacancies for the student. In many regions of the country there are no residential programs available, so that the family may have to approve sending the child to a program in another state. In spite of all these difficulties, families should consider residential programs when this seems in the best interest of the family and of the person with autism. Some states have made admirable progress in developing small residential programs for people with disabilities in local communities, and all states in the US are committed to developing more of these small programs in the future. Amy Lettick (1987) founder of Benhaven, has some excellent suggestions for families considering residential care for a child with autism, as well as ways for the family to evaluate residential programs to see if the program will meet the needs of the family member with autism.

Difficulties in the area of physical growth and development are not confined to medical and behavioral problems. If the teenager with autism is severely disabled, his or her physical development will soon outpace cognitive and emotional development. The parents may feel sorrow, and sometimes despair, as they see the other children in the family and the neighborhood progress through adolescence and prepare for a normal adult life.

(2) Fear and conflict about the future

Parents of children with autism do not always look to the future with hope. There are many realities that support this attitude. While the education of children with handicaps is mandated by law, there are no similar laws requiring services for most adults with handicaps. The child with autism who graduates from a high school special education program may not find any appropriate adult vocational or residential program available. Unfortunately, it is not uncommon for students with autism (and other handicaps) simply to remain at home doing nothing after they graduate from school at age twenty-one or twenty-two. This is a terrifying thought for many parents who see the hard-won educational and other gains from an intensive school program simply fading away. Most special education programs for school-age children encourage the development of educational goals and skills that will be useful for adult life. This approach is necessary, but can also result in conflict with parents. I have been to a number of IEP meetings where school staff members have proposed educational goals and objectives based on the assumption that all kinds of programs are available for adults with autism in the local community. In one meeting I attended, the teacher announced almost proudly that she had "no idea" what programs were available for adults in the local community even though her goals were based on the "future environment" of the student. It should have come as no surprise that the parents at the meeting were both amazed and angered by this statement. The best way to deal with this situation is not to ignore the future needs of the student with autism, and certainly not to limit educational goals because there are no appropriate adult programs available in the local community. But it is important for school staff members to understand the fear and anxiety that discussions of the future may provoke in parents who have a very realistic understanding of local conditions. Where there is a discussion of an ideal future for a student there should at least be an acknowledgment that the ideal is being discussed, and it would also be helpful to discuss ways of achieving the ideal, given the realities of the local situation.

As the adolescent with autism gets older, the family usually has to begin dealing with a totally different service system. The family is often comfortable with the local school and school staff after years of having children in the local schools. Even if the child with autism is placed in a residential program away from home, the parents generally become familiar with the residential staff, and comfortable with the program. Adult services for people with autism are usually funded and directed by state government agencies, or local nonprofit agencies that are monitored by the state. The adult programs usually have different admission requirements than school programs, and in some cases the adult program may place the person with autism on a waiting list for a considerable period of time. In order to be admitted to an adult program, a person with autism may have to receive funding through Title XIX (Medicaid) of the Social Security Act. In most cases the parents will have to apply for funding and deal with the complex, and sometimes incomprehensible, regulations of the Social Security Administration. An added frustration for parents is that the special education staff at their child's school may have little understanding of the requirements for admission to adult programs or of Title XIX funding.

Sex education is another area of potential conflict between families and school staff and other professionals. There has already been a discussion of the importance of some type of sex education training for all people with autism. This training has to be designed to meet the needs and level of understanding of the students. Some approaches to sex education (Ford, 1987) emphasize the importance of choice and respect the personal independence of the students with autism in the area of sexuality. There is nothing wrong with this approach, but there are times when parents may oppose certain types of sex education because the information conflicts with the moral or religious values of the family. While the professional carrying out of the sex education program may see the development of personal choice and independence as important for all people with autism, the family may agree that independence is important but also see the potential dangers associated with sexual behavior for the teenager or adult with autism. A further irritant for many families is that the professional can afford the luxury of theorizing about risk taking and making choices, but if the wrong choices are made by the family member with autism, the family, not the professional, will most likely face the consequences. Once again this is not an either-or situation. Successful sex education programs can provide the students with information they need, while at the same time recognizing the values and concerns of the family (see Ford, 1987), for a good discussion.

Sex education is not the only potential source of stress and conflict for the family and the teenager with autism. The process of transition from high school special education services to adult services for teenagers with handicaps is often a difficult time. Some high school special education programs place a great emphasis on preparing students for adult work, and in some cases, the students work for part of the school day in a job in the local community. This type of program is usually very appropriate for a student with autism, and it seems that students who have a good transition program are often more successful with employment as adults (Wilcox, McDonnell, Bellamy, and Rose, 1988). Even with very good programs, there is a chance for conflict and disagreement. Families may not place the same importance on work training as the educational program, and may in fact be strongly opposed to the idea that their son or daughter with autism should work in the community. In other situations, the family may want to develop work-training opportunities for their child with autism while the school staff may be unwilling or unable to provide an appropriate vocational program.

(3) Problems with brothers and sisters

Many of these issues have already been discussed in the previous chapter on families. It seems that the teenage years may bring additional difficulties for the brothers and sisters of an adolescent with autism. If the teenager with autism has severe limitations in intellectual or emotional development, the brothers and sisters may become embarrassed about recognizing the teenager as part of the family. This may be especially true if the siblings are also entering the teenage years when being accepted as a member of the group becomes so important. In the past, the brothers and sisters may have enjoyed playing with the sibling with autism, but as teenagers may not be comfortable including their handicapped sibling in their regular activities.

Other problems for siblings could include resentment or anger at the time spent by the parents caring for the teenager with autism. The siblings may also be apprehensive that they may be responsible for caring for their brother or sister once the parents are no longer able to carry out this responsibility. In some cases, the parents make it very clear that the brothers and sisters will be expected to take on this role. At other times, the siblings themselves wish to assume this role. In either case, the siblings probably have some concerns as to how this role of caring for a brother or sister who needs constant supervision or assistance will affect their own lives, careers, and marriages as adults.

It is very important to remember that not all siblings have unresolved problems dealing with their family situations. In my experience, many siblings manage very well, and conflicts and disagreements about caring for a teenager with autism are successfully handled by the family without any need for counseling or professional advice. At times family counseling may be requested, and the focus of the counseling could be on the right of the siblings to their own lives and activities, while at the same time the sibling might be expected to make some contribution to meeting the needs of the brother or sister with autism. Some siblings may find a sibling support group, or individual counseling, helpful.

Dealing with the Issues of Adolescence

It should be obvious from the discussions in the previous chapters that there are no solutions to problems for adolescents with autism that are appropriate for all individuals or all families. Very often there may be no simple solutions to any of the problems. Still, there are approaches in working together with families that I think may be helpful for many families struggling with these issues and problems.

The approach for dealing with problems in adolescence presented by families and teenagers with autism is the same basic strategy discussed in the previous chapter on working with families.

(1) Clarify the problem

This is a basis for any form of effective counseling. Some suggestions for helping the family members get some understanding of basis of problems or conflicts have already been discussed. In the teenage years there seems to be a greater chance of conflict and misunderstanding within families, as well as between families and schools and other service agencies, around such issues as dealing with behavior problems in the home, sex education, planning for the future, and the possible need for residential placement. These conflicts are often difficult to clarify. The conflict may be the result not only of different values and moral perspectives, but also of feelings of being overwhelmed and helpless. At times the parents or the brothers and sisters of a teenager with autism face so many problems at once they may be tempted to withdraw from the activities of the local community along with the teenager. This leads to social isolation, and the family has even fewer resources in the form of family, friends, and neighbors, to help in times of need or crisis.

(2) Exploration of feelings

People sometimes ask for professional help not because they want a way out of their problems, but because they simply want someone to listen to them. The chance to express openly and explore feelings about the issues or conflict can be valuable for all members of the family.

Most counselors and other helping professionals will recognize the importance of dealing with the feelings around an issue. But the expression of feelings should not necessarily be an end in itself. A few families and family members might just want the chance to express their feelings and nothing more from the counselor, and this should be respected. In most cases, I found that families wanted and expected the counselor or other professional to be able to help in the area of practical problem solving. We have all heard about the counseling or therapy that seems to go on for years with all kinds of feelings being explored, but no practical results to show for time or money spent. Families with a teenager with autism who seek professional help are often faced with so many immediate, practical difficulties that they usually will have little patience with a counselor or other professional whose only approach is the constant rehashing of feelings over a long period of time.

An important part of the exploration of feelings that some counselors try to avoid are the questions of meaning and faith. Even families with strong religious commitments may find themselves with feelings of despair and hopelessness, especially when trying to cope with the problems of adolescence and autism. A referral to a member of the clergy or a pastoral counselor may be appropriate if the counselor feels uncomfortable in dealing with these questions.

(3) Explore possible options

This does not mean a long theoretical discussion of possible services for a teenager with autism. The basis of this discussion should be the unique and individual skills, needs, and situation of the teenager with autism and of his or her family. If the counselor feels that his or her knowledge of autism is not adequate to help the family realistically explore options, a referral to another counselor or professional is one possibility. Another possibility is for the counselor and the family to explore possible options together. In fact, it may be a benefit not to have too many preconceived notions about autism before starting this process. The book by Turnbull, Turnbull, Bronicki, Summers, and Roeder-Gordon (1989) is a very comprehensive guide to planning for the future of a teenager with disabilities. This book contains a number of checklists to help the family focus on the unique preferences, needs, and skills of the teenager with autism or other handicaps, along with a wealth of information on practical matters to do with preparing for adult services. I believe that a counselor could use this or a similar book as the basis for a productive working relationship with a family.

(4) Take action

It is often difficult to get from the discussion stage of a counseling relationship to the stage of taking practical action to help deal with the problem. Yet if these actions are not taken, much of the information and effort invested in the counseling relationship has been wasted. The actions taken will obviously depend on the options generated during the previous phase of the counseling relationship. Often, after some actions have been taken, the options may have to be reexamined to see how realistic they were, and other options developed. The book by Turnbull et al. (1989) discussed above, has a number of good suggestions for action. These suggestions will have to be adapted to the local situation and the needs of the particular family and the teenager with autism.

At the action stage, help is often needed from others who may have been through the same experience, or who have the necessary professional knowledge or political contacts. This emphasizes again the importance of social support, the emotional and practical support given by friends, neighbors, and acquaintances. Many counselors and others will provide a very valuable service to a family by helping that family become linked to others who are experiencing the same needs or problems. Friends and neighbors who know nothing about autism but are willing to listen and help can also be a great help to a family. This help is not only psychological. A study of adults with disabilities found that these adults were more likely to find jobs through informal contacts made by them or their families, than through contacts provided by various agencies (Bellamy, Rhodes, Mank, and Albin, 1988, p. 227). A good social support network will be available for a family long after the professionals have left the scene.

The counselor may have to take some responsibility for tracking down financial or other support needed by the family. Ideally, the family members should be supported as they do this for themselves, but the human services system can be so complex that the family may need advice and support from a professional. Possible sources of information and support would be the local office of the agency responsible for serving people with developmental disabilities in the community, or advocacy or parent groups affiliated with the Autism Society of America or similar organizations, or general referral agencies that are run by United Way or various state governments in many regions. About twenty states now offer cash assistance payments to some families with children with disabilities living with them (Agosta, 1989), and these programs are usually administered through the state agency responsible for developmental disabilities. Families who meet the strict income requirements may also be eligible to receive Medicaid and Supplemental Security Income (SSI) payments through the Social Security Administration.

Special education programs for high school students with autism and other disabilities are now required to develop transition plans to help students move from the school system to the adult services network. A good transition plan will include many of the resources discussed above, and have educational goals that are designed to help the student become as independent as possible in adult life (see Halvorsen, Doering, Farron-Davis, Usilton and Sailor, 1989, for a good discussion). The school special education staff can be a great source of information and emotional support for the family facing the transition of a teenager from adolescence to adult life, as well as a resource for the counselor working with the family.

(5) Evaluate the action

There are few simple and direct solutions to any of the problems faced by people with autism or members of their families. Not every action will be successful, so it is important to keep track of actions taken, and the results of those actions. This is not to assess blame when certain actions fail, but to use failure as a learning experience. Perhaps the options that formed the basis of the action were too narrow or too broad. Was the action implemented with the right person, at the right time, in the right manner? Was the action implemented at all?

After the success or failure of an action, the next question is, where do we go from here? The next stage may be to reevaluate the options, or to take other actions, or perhaps even to end the counseling relationship. If there is a decision to end the counseling relationship, the family and the counselor together may decide that a referral to another professional might be best, or that the family will consult the counselor on an as-needed basis. In some cases the family members will decide they need no further professional help. Some counselors will be sad or even angry at this last decision. Often however this decision not to seek further professional help is the best possible outcome of the counseling relationship. If as a result of a counseling relationship a family or an individual with autism has become more aware of their own coping skills and abilities, and is confident enough to take action to meet their own needs, the counselor has done a good job. Whatever happens, experienced counselors realize that the process of counseling and helping is not a matter of arriving at cut-and-dried solutions, but an ongoing process of trial and error with a mixture of successes and failures for everyone in the counseling relationship.

Summary

Adolescence can be a difficult time for a teenager with autism and his or her family, just as it can be difficult for any person. Not every adolescent, or every family, needs professional assistance during this time. But it is more likely for families, and sometimes teenagers with autism, to seek professional help during the adolescent years. The type and amount of help needed will vary according to the unique needs of the teenager and the family.

Further Information

There is a growing interest in the needs of teenagers with autism and their families as they prepare for adult life. Some recent publications are very helpful even if they discuss disabilities in general and do not necessarily focus on autism. Halvorsen et al. (1989) discuss transition programs from school to adult programs for students with severe disabilities. The best general introduction to preparing for adult life for teenagers with disabilities is the book by Turnbull et al. (1989): this book has a wealth of practical information on every important aspect of preparing for adult life. It would be a great resource for families and counselors interested in the topic.

6

Adults with Autism

I guess I won't be around to take care of her much longer.
                    —Father of young woman with autism.

O ver the past thirty years there has been tremendous progress in the development of services and programs for adults with autism. Thirty years ago the vast
majority of adults were placed in large state institutions,
or were cared for at home by the family with little or
no support. In some states, even the large institutions refused to accept adults with autism for admission, creating
desperate, and sometimes tragic, situations for families.
Now there is a greatly expanded service system for both
children and adults with autism. New options are available
for semi-independent and independent living in the local
community, and even those adults who are severely handicapped with autism and mental retardation are successfully working and earning money (Sullivan, 1987).

In spite of the progress, there are still significant problems in obtaining services for adults with autism in many
areas of the country. In some regions, residential and vocational programs for adults may be inadequate or nonexistent. Families who are used to special education for
children with autism as a right under Public Law 94–142,
are often dismayed to find there is no similar entitlement
to services for adults with autism. Where services for
adults are available the family may be forced to place the

adult on a long waiting list for a residential or day program. If the adult program is inadequate, the family may experience a "take or leave it" attitude from the program staff because there are so few programs for adults available. Sometimes the family becomes so desperate that its members will accept any program because the services are so inadequate in a region.

In addition to problems obtaining services, the family may also have problems understanding the whole new service system it is involved with once its family member with autism becomes an adult. Children with autism are educated at the expense of the local school system and the state. Funding for adult services generally comes from a wide variety of sources, including Title XIX of the Social Security Act. These sources of funding have complex regulations. In some cases, the family financial assets will be reviewed and any money or assets inherited by, or placed in trust for, the adult with autism could affect eligibility for benefits. Families may need the services of an attorney and a financial planner or accountant familiar with disability issues to help untangle the funding maze for adult services. The book by Turnbull et al. (1989) has an excellent discussion of the issues around Medicaid, Social Security, and other sources of funding. Local advocacy groups, such as the Autism Society of America, or the Association for Retarded Citizens, may also have good information on adult programs and funding.

Families and adults with autism may also experience many of the conflicts that young adults experience with their parents and other members of the family. Disagreements and misunderstandings around such issues as autonomy, how to behave and dress, and sexual expression, are not uncommon in many families. The existence of these disagreements within a family does not necessarily suggest that the family needs, or wants, professional counseling.

Like adolescence, adulthood should not be thought of

as a time of constant conflict and disagreement. In some cases, certain types of compulsive behaviors associated with autism become less severe when the individual becomes an adult (Paul, 1987, p. 123). It is important to remember that even adults with autism who are severely handicapped are still capable throughout their lives of learning new skills.

Issues for Adults with Autism and Their Families

The issues faced by adults and their families will vary according to individual situations and circumstances. There are some issues that I found that many families and individual adults with autism seem to face.

(1) Autonomy

The struggle to be independent, and to face up to the rights and responsibilities of adult life, confronts most young adults at one time or another. Where there is a family member who is an adult with autism, the parents and siblings may have mixed feelings about the autonomy that adult life is supposed to bring. Especially if the individual with autism needs constant care and supervision, the family members may be appropriately concerned that the adult with autism not be placed in a situation where he or she can be abused or exploited. This often is a concern in the area of sexuality and sexual expression. If the adult is living in the community independently or semi-independently, and working with nonhandicapped people all day, the family may be concerned that there are much greater chances for exploitation of the person with handicaps than in more restrictive residences and day programs where there are staff people who are familiar with autism. Some adults with autism have serious behavior problems such as assault or self-injury, and the family may also be concerned that a member of the public could be injured if there is a problem in a public place or at a job site. There are also times when the family may feel that the residential or day program is not giving the adult enough autonomy, and the professionals and program staff are being overprotective.

The parents of an adult with autism may also find their own autonomy restricted. Many parents, especially parents of a child with severe handicaps who will probably need care for life, assume that they automatically become that child's legal guardian when the child becomes an adult. In fact, parents usually have to petition a court to be appointed their adult family member's legal guardian. This is not usually a difficult process, but the parents then realize that many of the decisions they make for their child can be reviewed by a judge or other advocate. At times, the decisions of parents who are legal guardians have been overturned by the courts. I do not believe this is always a bad situation: there are cases where parents or other legal guardians have not lived up to their responsibilities. Even so, this scrutiny by courts or other agencies can make parents and family members nervous, and in some cases resentful. Some families argue that they often have been solely responsible for providing care for the member of the family with autism, they have been forced to struggle through difficult times with little support, and they resent being "second-guessed" by someone who might have little understanding of their particular situation. Although I do not completely agree with this point of view, it is easy to see how difficult the situation can be for many parents.

There is no quick and easy way to resolve differences and disagreements around the issue of autonomy. The individual rights and preferences of the adult with autism must be respected. At the same time, there needs to be some consideration given to the feelings and preferences of the family. I think this is especially important if the adult with autism is living in the family home, and the family will have to deal with any consequences of the adult's use of his or her autonomy. It is not usually productive to deal with this situation as a conflict between the rights of the adult with autism and of his or her family. Most families manage to cope with these disagreements without professional help. If professional counseling is requested, I think the most useful approach, depending on the needs of the individual and the family, is a compromise where the adult with autism can gain more independence and autonomy, while the realistic concerns of the family are also addressed.

(2) *Concern about the future*

If the person with autism is likely to need special care for life, it is understandable that parents will usually be very concerned about the future, especially what happens after the death or disability of one or both parents. To add to this concern is the reality in most cases that siblings have moved out of the home and started their own families. Although the brothers and sisters genuinely care about their sibling with autism, they also have their own families as their major priorities.

Some parents deal with these concerns by placing their son or daughter with autism in the best possible residential and day program, and hoping that the program will be around for the life of the person. Parents have founded their own residential and day programs if no suitable programs were available locally, not only as a way of ensuring proper care of their own son or daughter but also as a way of providing services for other individuals with autism in the area. Founding a program is not a quick and easy solution to this problem; however, a number of parents have successfully started programs for children and adults with autism in the United States and overseas. Other parents may wish to advocate for the expansion of current programs in order to have the necessary education and residence for their son or daughter.

In addition to having their son or daughter with autism established in a good residential and vocational program, parents may also wish to make financial and legal plans to protect the person with autism after the death of the parents. This can be accomplished through wills and various trust documents. Those who wish to establish trusts and wills to provide for legal guardianship and some financial support for an adult with autism need to be aware that this can be a very complex area of financial planning and legal practice. It is essential to make use of attorneys and accountants or financial planners who are up to date and aware of the many issues surrounding Social Security and legal guardianship. These issues are different from state to state, and can change dramatically over time. Competent legal and financial advice is essential since an improperly worded trust document or legal guardianship arrangement may result in the persons not being eligible for certain financial benefits, and ultimately do more harm than good (see Turnbull et al., 1989, pp. 81–156, and Apolloni, 1989, for excellent discussions of these issues).

An interesting new type of program has been recently developed that may be helpful to many parents as they plan the future care of an adult with disabilities. In a number of states and regions, case-management services provided by nonprofit corporations could provide individual oversight and management of the services needed by an adult with autism or other disabilities. The case-management agency does not, and should not, provide vocational or residential services, but will help to ensure that appropriate services are available to the adult with disabilities, and that financial resources are being used in the best interest of the person. Many state agencies also provide case-management services for adults with developmental disabilities, but although these services are valuable, the case manager for the state agency may have a case load of forty to fifty persons and be unable to provide the attention necessary to monitor regularly the needs of a particular person. The nonprofit case-management organizations usually deal with smaller numbers of people, although they do have costs that the family must meet. Apolloni (1989) has a description of nonprofit case-management programs (sometimes known as corporate guardianship programs), as well as a listing of these programs in the United States.

(3) Obtaining services

As noted previously in this chapter, adult services can be difficult to obtain for many families. Day and residential programs may have long waiting lists, while in-home support programs and parent counseling and support groups are often oriented toward the needs of parents with preschool or school-age children.

A counselor who is asked to help a family with an adult family member with autism could find that the parents and nonhandicapped siblings are overwhelmed by the many problems they face, and are close to exhaustion and despair. It is not the task or responsibility of the counselor to wave a magic wand and resolve all these difficulties at once. Counselors who have these "rescuer" fantasies will soon become frustrated and cynical themselves unless they are aware of their own needs, strengths, and limitations. Most families who have lived with these complex problems for years will be appropriately dubious of any counselor or other professional who seems to promise quick and easy solutions to problems.

I think that the most useful service a counselor can provide is to give the family members a chance to express their feelings, clarify the issues faced by the family, help the family assess not only family problems but sources of support and strength for the family, make reasonable priorities of what needs to be done, take action, and evaluate the actions. In the process of obtaining services, the family will probably need to assess the individual needs and preferences of the adult with autism, discuss family expectations for services, and examine options for obtaining the needed services. The process of taking action may begin slowly by having the family apply for Social Security and other financial assistance that may be available to help care for an adult with autism at home. The family members may draw on a network of friends, neighbors, and relatives to find a part-time job for the person with autism. If a job is not available, some type of appropriate volunteer work could be helpful in getting the person out of the house and learning the routine skills of following directions, completing tasks, and cooperating with others. Members of the family may wish to join other families in advocacy groups and lobby for increased residential and day services in their local area. As discussed previously, some families could band together to form a nonprofit corporation to develop an appropriate adult residential or vocational program for their sons and daughters.

(4) Is there any place for me?

Most of this chapter has been concerned with counseling parents and other family members of adults with autism. There are of course adults with autism who are verbal with normal or above-normal intelligence who have many of the difficulties with social relationships and the use of language associated with the syndrome of autism. These adults may have acute feelings of being different and isolated from the regular community, and they may seek professional counseling.

No one type of counseling or other service is appropriate for all people with autism. There is always the requirement that the counseling fit the needs and situation of the individual. In general, however, counseling of verbal adults with autism would probably be most effective if focused on immediate, concrete issues such as getting along with parents, roommates, or coworkers, dating and making friends, dealing with stress and frustration, etc. The counselor should be aware of the possibility of depression or other psychiatric conditions along with the syndrome of autism. Dealing with autism and other psychiatric conditions can be complex and difficult even for the most experienced counselor, and consultation with an experienced psychiatrist is almost always necessary.

The most appropriate counseling interventions for verbal adults with autism seem to be behavioral social skills training and very focused and concrete supportive counseling (Kilman and Negri-Shoultz, 1987; Riddle, 1987). Some of the cognitive behavior modification procedures such as self-instructional procedures (Meichenbaum, 1975), as well as support groups, may also be helpful for certain adults with autism. Generally, counseling approaches that rely on open-ended and relatively unstructured exploration of feelings typical of many of the psychoanalytic therapies will probably not be helpful in counseling adults with autism, and may even be counter productive in some circumstances. Once again, it is important to remember that people with autism are individuals, so it is important not to rule out completely approaches or therapies simply on the basis of a diagnosis of autism.

Just as the goal of counseling families is to support that family's own coping skills and support networks, counseling adults with autism should be focused on the development of the person's unique skills and abilities, and to help the person develop a network of others willing and able to provide support in the future.

Dealing with the Issues of the Adult with Autism

The counseling approach consistently taken throughout this book has emphasized not only the importance of expressing and recognizing feelings about situations and issues, but using these feelings to develop concrete plans of action. In my experience, most families and individuals with autism who seek counseling will expect more than a ventilation of their feelings on a particular issue or situation. Programs for children and adults with autism that are known to be effective, such as Division TEACCH, place a great emphasis on an attitude from professionals that encourages the sharing of honest feelings, but also stresses the importance of practical action as a follow-up to the expression of feelings (Marcus and Schopler, 1987, pp. 499–502).

A counseling relationship with an adult with autism, or with his or her family members, will usually be most effective if it follows the sequence discussed in detail in the previous chapters. This sequence is:

(1) Clarification of the issues;
(2) Expression of feelings around the issues;
(3) Consideration of options available to deal with the situation;
(4) Take action based on the options;
(5) Evaluate the effectiveness of the actions and return to earlier stages of the process if necessary.

Summary

Great progress has been made in recent years in developing services for adults with autism. Much still needs to be done. Adult programs for people with autism are not available in some regions of the country, and other programs have long waiting lists. The literature on services for children with autism and the needs of families with children with autism considerably outweigh the information on the needs of adults and their families. This situation is changing, especially with the growth of small residences for adults in local communities and the development of such programs as supported employment even for adults who are severely disabled with autism.

The gaps in current services for adults should not blind us to the progress that has been made, and is continuing at present. Ruth Sullivan (1987) a parent, professional, and advocate in the field of autism for over twenty years, described the situation for services for adults and children with autism very well: "The winds of change are clearing the dark skies in many places. Services are getting better—slowly, slowly—but better, nonetheless" (p. 742).

Further Information

A good, general overview of the issues around autism in adolescents and adults is provided in the book edited by Schopler and Mesibov (1983). A very practical and helpful discussion of the needs of adults with disabilities for parents and professionals is the book by Turnbull et al. (1989). For a comprehensive discussion of employment programs for adults with autism see McCarthy, Fender, and Fender (1988).

7

Medication*

Children and adults with autism often experience symptoms of emotional and behavioral disturbance, and may, in fact, be at increased risk for the development of secondary neuropsychiatric disorders (including disorders of mood and affect). In these cases, the use of a psychotropic medication (those medications designed to change mood or behavior), can be an important part of the overall treatment plan.

Recent Controversies

During recent years, controversy has surrounded the use of psychotropic medications for people with autism and other developmental disorders. The reasons for this controversy are complex, reflecting both philosophical and practical issues and concerns. Opponents of medication argue that autism is a developmental disorder that is not amenable to such treatment, that individuals with autism are in some way protected from developing other, more common, neuropsychiatric disorders, and that medications are typically used in excessive doses and in place of appropriate educational programming. There is some basis in truth for these beliefs, especially concerning some of the past practices common in the field of developmental

*This chapter was written by Joel Bregman, M.D.

disabilities. There was inadequate educational, vocational, and rehabilitative programming in many large institutions; the institutions themselves could be dehumanizing places; staffing was often so inadequate that no appropriate programs could be carried out; physicians were not adequately trained in the needs of the developmentally disabled population; the physician was often not considered part of the treatment-planning team; and there was a limited body of research knowledge regarding the response of individuals with autism to various medications.

Although the concern about the use of psychotropic medication certainly is valid and appropriate, overly restrictive viewpoints and policies often lead to withholding of potentially valuable treatment, and restrict the quality of life of the individuals the policies were designed to protect.

Appropriate Use of Psychotropic Medication

These issues and concerns can be addressed in a productive manner. Advocates for people with autism and other disabilities have already begun the effort to ensure the development of intensive, well-structured, and functionally based educational, vocational, and residential programs. Future directions should also include increased support for the education and training of physicians (psychiatrists, pediatricians, and neurologists) in the assessment and treatment of people with autism and other developmental disabilities. Advocacy groups and counselors and other professionals in allied fields could aid this effort by offering to provide lectures, seminars, and training sites for physicians and medical students. This will have the added benefit of increasing the likelihood that the physician will become an active part of the program-planning team, and become informed and involved in clinical situations *before* a crisis develops. Certainly, there is a great need of expanded programs of research that address the biological, psychological, behavioral, and educational aspects of developmental disabilities. The knowledge resulting from this increased research should lead to substantially improved treatment approaches, obviating unnecessary treatment trials and potential side effects. Parents and advocates need to advise legislative, governmental, and community officials of the importance of support (both financial and professional) for basic and applied research in this field.

Strategies to ensure the best use of medication

Although there are many gaps in our knowledge of autism, we now know from current research and clinical experience that a number of children and adults with autism can benefit appreciably from the use of medication. There are no known medications or treatments that will "cure" or reverse the effects of autism. But medication should be considered for children and adults with autism where there are severe behavioral problems that are not responding to appropriate behavior modification or educational programs, or where there are secondary neuropsychiatric disorders that are potentially harmful or seriously interfere with adaptive growth or development (for example, severe depression).

There is also evidence that medications can improve the tolerance of social contact for some persons with autism, and that certain medications may make some individuals more responsive to educational and behavioral programming. In some research studies, the use of medication has increased the effectiveness of the behavior modification program.

The presence of certain symptoms should suggest that medication be considered in many cases. These symptoms include hyperactivity, inattentiveness, impulsivity, low frustration tolerance, aggressive behavior, temper outbursts, and agitation. Professionals have become increasingly aware of an apparent increased risk for the development of secondary neuropsychiatric disorders among those with autism. For instance, several groups of researchers and clinicians reported that cyclic disturbances of mood and affect similar to bipolar manic-depressive disorder are not uncommon. In these instances a symptom cluster involving giddy, silly, hyperirritable moods, substantially decreased sleep and appetite, hyperactive, impulsive behavior, and other behavioral excesses (such as stereotypic, self-injurious, or aggressive behavior) alternate with periods of relative calm and contentment: there also may be a symptom cluster involving unhappy, tearful moods, substantially increased or decreased sleep or appetite, decreased energy, and a lack of enjoyment and interest in usually preferred activities. Most recently, attention has been focused on a potential association between autism and Tourette's Syndrome, a movement disorder that includes simple and complex motor and vocal tics. In *some* cases, repetitive movements or vocalizations may actually represent involuntary tics rather than stereotypic behaviors so typical of autism. Preliminary research studies suggest that medication treatment directed toward these associated disorders may be beneficial for some individuals with autism.

It is also possible that other symptom clusters that occur rather frequently among people with autism, such as complex, compulsive behaviors, may share common biological features with recognized neuropsychiatric disorders such as obsessive compulsive disorder, and respond favorably to appropriate treatment. Further research will be necessary in order to answer these questions.

Assessment for medication

It follows from the discussion above that decisions regarding medication treatment should be preceded by a complete neuropsychiatric evaluation. This evaluation should include a complete review of current and past affective and behavioral symptoms and treatment interventions, a functional analysis of behavior, and a review of medical, development, educational, and family histories. Family history is most important, since some neuropsychiatric disorders have a familial or genetic component and may affect other children in the family with or without developmental disabilities. Obtaining information from day and residential teachers, or other staff members familiar with the person with autism, is extremely important. After this process of information gathering, several interview and/or observation sessions should be held with the student or the client. Ideally, some of these sessions should be conducted at the day and residential programs, so that naturalistic observations of behavior and interpersonal interactions can be made.

Conducting a medication trial

If a medication trial seems indicated, it should be conducted in as systematic a manner as possible, for a number of reasons. First, among people with autism, affective and behavioral disturbances are often cyclic, with periods of adaptive and relatively productive functioning alternating with periods of maladaptive, unproductive functioning. In some cases, improved behavior that occurs following the initiation of medication may be related to a natural period of improvement rather than to a direct medication effect. Second, medication is usually considered at a time of crisis, when a number of ecological, programmatic, and behavioral interventions also are being initiated. Often it is unclear which intervention or combination of interventions is actually responsible for behavioral improvement. Third, even among individuals with autism, placebo effects occur. In this situation, a placebo effect refers to changes in the environment or attitudes of staff or parents toward the person with autism. When a child or adult with autism is having a difficult time, there is frequently greater personal attention paid to the individual; staff and parents may thus expect to see positive behavior changes, and overall there may be a different way of interacting with the person with autism. The behavior may change for the better, but the medication may have had no role in the behavior change, or the behavior may not really change at all but parents and staff report positive effects because this is what they were expecting to happen. Finally, the medication may give the person with autism a different feeling (for example, may make the person feel drowsy), and this feeling may result in a behavior change; the change was not really due to the intended therapeutic effect of the medication.

The most systematic treatment approach ideally would involve participation in a research study that includes a placebo condition and a "double blind." A placebo in this situation is an inactive substance or treatment that looks like the regular medication (sometimes called a "sugar pill"). "Double blind" refers to a lack of knowledge by the patient, family, staff, or physician of exactly when the active medication and the placebo are being taken, until the study is completed. Using these procedures substantially reduces the possibility that an observed treatment response is due to high expectations and anticipation rather than to a true medication effect. In many cases it is not possible to conduct a double-blind study. Another approach would be a systematic clinical trial that involves a baseline period of data collection (using accurate and reliable methods of observation, symptom checklists, etc.), followed by a medication period. If the medication leads to improvement then using periods of medication withdrawal and reinstitution should follow. This approach should help to increase the confidence that positive changes in mood or behavior can really be attributed to the medication.

This process of thorough assessment and treatment requires the participation of a knowledgeable and invested physician who can work with a treatment team and accept modest clinical gains without becoming overly discouraged. The best way to find such a physician would be through the psychiatry or developmental pediatrics department of a university medical center. Clinicians and clinical investigators experienced in autism and other developmental disabilities are often faculty members within departments of child and adolescent psychiatry. The development of close ties between such a department and an educational or vocational program for children or adults with autism can be beneficial and enriching for all concerned. Other potential sources of referrals for physicians include the American Academy of Child and Adolescent Psychiatry, the American Academy of Pediatrics, and local and state medical, psychiatric, and pediatric associations.

Specific Medications

A wide variety of psychotropic medications have been reported to offer clinical benefit for at least some individuals with autism. Unfortunately, there have been relatively few carefully conducted studies regarding the efficacy and potential side effects of specific medications within the autistic population. Therefore, there is little scientific information regarding the factors (for example, age, specific symptoms, etc.) that would predict a beneficial response for a particular medication in a given client or patient. Scientific research in this area needs to be encouraged and supported.

Prior to a medication trial, a medical evaluation should be performed. This may include a physical and neurological examination, and appropriate laboratory and clinical tests. All medications are associated with undesirable effects, some of them potentially serious, so the possible risks and benefits of a particular treatment should be discussed in detail with the prescribing physician. The following discussion of specific medications includes a description of common side effects; however, a variety of other side effects are possible.

Neuroleptics

Neuroleptics are the class of medications variously referred to as neuroleptics, antipsychotics, or major tranquilizers. This class of medication has received the most intensive study for use with people with autism. Within this class, haloperidol (Haldol and others) has received the most scrutiny, but several other related medications have also been studied, such as trifluoperazine (Stelazine and others), thiothixene (Navane and others), chlorpromazine (Thorazine and others), and thioridazine (Mellaril and others). The neuroleptic medications are particularly beneficial in the treatment of schizophrenia and other psychotic disorders, mania, and the tic disorder known as Tourette's Syndrome. These medications also seem to be appropriate for some people with autism. One of the major neurochemical actions of the neuroleptics is the blocking of the dopamine neurochemical system of the brain, a system closely involved in motor behavior, thought process, and emotions. The rationale for the initial neuroleptic trials with individuals with autism included similarities in the symptoms and behavioral features of autism and some psychotic conditions, and the erroneous assumption that autism may represent early onset schizophrenia. Although these rationales seem rather weak, the fact remains that neuroleptics have proven to be quite helpful for a number of children and adults with autism.

Several well-conducted, scientifically sound research studies indicate that these medications (particularly haloperidol) can be very beneficial for some individuals with autism in reducing behavioral symptoms such as hyperactivity, impulsivity, stereotypy, and social withdrawal. Some studies suggest that learning performance may be impaired as a result of these medications, especially with the more sedating members of the class (such as thioridazine and chlorpromazine). However, other studies using haloperidol have shown that some types of learning actually may improve. Since clinically beneficial effects are typically achieved with relatively low doses of these medications, short-term side effects are usually minimal. The most common short-term side effects include sedation, restlessness, muscle spasm, slowed movements, dry mouth, constipation, and blurred vision. A more serious (but *infrequent*) side effect has been reported, called neuroleptic malignant syndrome. This condition includes fever, confusion, elevation of white blood cell counts and liver enzymes, muscle tissue breakdown, and potential kidney damage. When identified early, serious complications can be avoided.

Of more serious concern is the development of a potentially irreversible movement disorder, called tardive dyskinesia. Tardive dyskinesia occurs in as many as 20 to 25 percent of those who are treated with neuroleptics over time. Tardive dyskinesia involves rapid, involuntary movements of various muscle groups of the body, most frequently affecting the tongue, mouth, and facial muscles. It usually begins with mild symptoms that progress if the neuroleptics are not tapered off and discontinued. If discovered early, many of the movements will disappear or decrease in severity over time. This movement disorder typically develops following many years of continuous treatment with neuroleptics, and is at least partially related to the total amount of medication an individual receives in his or her lifetime. It is very unusual, but not unheard of, for tardive dyskinesia to develop after only a few months of treatment, particularly in younger male patients. Even after several months of treatment, movements of tardive dyskinesia can occur *temporarily* in as many as 20 percent of patients following discontinuation of the neuroleptics (particularly abrupt discontinuation). The risks of tardive dyskinesia can be minimized by using the lowest *therapeutic* dose of the neuroleptics, and reserving their use for particularly distressful and interfering symptoms and behaviors.

Fenfluramine

Fenfluramine has received much systematic study in the past few years. The major clinical use of fenfluramine has been in weight reduction, since it typically reduces appetite rather substantially. The rationale for its use in autism stems from its ability to reduce the levels of the neurochemical, serotonin, circulating in the bloodstream. It has been known for many years that about one-third of individuals with autism have elevated levels of serotonin, although the significance of this finding remains obscure. The relationship between serotonin in the bloodstream and serotonin in the brain remains unknown. An initial report on the effects of fenfluramine in autism was published about eight years ago, and suggested that significant improvements in intellectual, social, and behavioral functioning may result from treatment. This preliminary report involved relatively few children with autism and was not a double-blind study with placebo. Since that time, a relatively large number of double-blind, placebo-controlled studies have been performed, including a large multicenter collaborative effort. The results of these larger studies have been substantially less encouraging than the original report. Some of the children in the study (about one-quarter to one-third of the subjects), experienced behavioral improvement involving the symptoms of hyperactivity, impulsivity, and stereotypy, however, intellectual, language, and social functioning remained essentially unchanged. An interesting finding of these studies was that neither a high baseline serotonin level, nor a substantial decrease in serotonin levels during treatment, predicted a favorable response to the medication. Although some reports indicated that younger, more intellectually competent individuals with autism were more likely to respond favorably to fenfluramine, other studies have not confirmed these associations. Some side effects are relatively common and include sedation, appetite reduction, at least temporary weight loss, and irritability. Some concern has been raised about possible brain damage resulting from the use of fenfluramine, since some animals given very large amounts of this medication show indications of such damage. There have been no reports of brain damage occurring in humans.

Lithium

As mentioned earlier in this chapter, there recently has been a growing awareness of the possibility of cyclic disturbances of mood, affect, and behavior among some people with autism. There are suggestions that the frequency of these bipolar manic-depressive type of disturbances may be higher within the autistic population than in the general population, although more formal study is necessary. Recently, several case reports have been published that suggested a medication known to be effective for bipolar manic-depressive disorder, lithium carbonate, may be helpful for those with autism who have similar affective and behavioral symptoms. Lithium is a salt that is effective in approximately three-quarters of bipolar patients in stabilizing mood and affect, normalizing sleep, appetite, and energy level, and reducing psychotic symptoms. It also has a prophylactic effect, that is, the ability to reduce the likelihood of future episodes. It is usually well tolerated by patients, but side effects are not uncommon and can include increased thirst and urination, a fine tremor of the hands, weight gain and fluid retention, a disturbance of the body's salt and water balance, and with long-term use, suppression of the thyroid gland. The latter problem can be corrected by discontinuation of lithium, or if continued lithium treatment is called for, the addition of thyroid medication. There has been some concern that with long-term use (of more than five to ten years), lithium may decrease the ability of the kidney to excrete concentrated urine, but this has not been proven. A trial of lithium may prove beneficial as part of the treatment of a person with autism who also has a cyclic mood disturbance.

Opioid antagonists

There has been increasing interest in a class of medications, the so-called opioid antagonists (such as naltrexone), particularly in the treatment of serious self-injurious behavior among individuals with mental retardation, including those with autism. This group of medications blocks the activity of the brain's natural narcoticlike system. Many of the functions of this "endogenous opioid system" are not understood; however, it is known that the perception of pain is mediated, at least in part, by this system. In addition, some animal studies suggest that the opioid system may be involved in social attachment behavior between infant animals and their mothers. The opioid antagonists are being studied for use in a wide variety of illnesses and disorders (including eating disorders and autism), but their main use has been in the treatment of narcotic addiction. Once the individual addicted to narcotics has been successfully withdrawn from these drugs, an opioid blocker (antagonist) such as naltrexone can help maintain abstinence, since the effects of narcotics are blocked by the antagonist. The rationale for trials of opioid blockers in developmental disabilities includes an attempt to alter pain perception and, perhaps, attachment behavior. Many individuals with developmental disabilities who are self-injurious seem to experience an unusually high tolerance for painful stimuli. Since the opioid blockers decrease the pain threshold, that is, increase an individual's perception of pain, they may help decrease self-injurious behavior. In addition, it has been *suggested* that self-injurious behavior may be self-perpetuating because some pleasure may be obtained from the release of natural narcoticlike substances that follows a painful experience. The use of an opioid blocker would eliminate this possible pleasurable experience, and may lead to a reduction in the self-injurious behavior.

The other rationale for trials of the opioid antagonists in autism follows from the animal research discussed above. Opioid blockers appear to increase the distress that infant animals experience when they are separated from their mothers. Since a primary disturbance of autism involves deficient social relatedness, the use of an opioid blocker *might* increase attachment behavior. This rationale is based on educated guesses (hypotheses) from animal studies; there are no studies that prove this hypothesis is true for humans with autism. The use of these medications should, therefore, be considered experimental. Several trials of opioid blockers have been conducted with small numbers of individuals with mental retardation and autism, principally for the treatment of serious self-injurious behavior. Both naloxone (given by injection), and naltrexone (given by mouth) have been used. The results of these studies have been quite mixed: favorable results have been reported in some studies but not in others. Further study is needed. There appear to be relatively few side effects related to the use of naltrexone. Reversible inflammation of the liver does occur in some patients, especially at higher doses. Liver function should be monitored during treatment.

Beta-blockers

Another class of medications that has received considerable attention over recent years for the treatment of behavioral problems among individuals with mental retardation and autism is the group known as beta-blockers. These medications block the so-called beta-adrenergic receptors that are part of the adrenaline system of the body. The oldest and most frequently prescribed beta-blocker is propranolol (Inderal and others). The beta-blockers have wide-ranging effects involving many different systems of the body and they are used for a correspondingly large number of medical conditions. They are used most often in the treatment of high blood pressure, some heart rhythm disturbances, anginal heart pain, migraine headaches, essential tremor, and during the time of a heart attack. The beta-blockers are also capable of reducing many of the physical symptoms of anxiety, such as fast, pounding heartbeat, flushing, and sweating. In addition, a few well-conducted studies suggest that the beta-blockers may be helpful for some individuals who experience explosive, aggressive outbursts following a serious brain injury. This latter observation led to the speculation that beta-blockers may be helpful for those persons with mental retardation who exhibit explosive episodes involving aggressive and destructive behavior. To date there have been a number of case studies attesting to the potential benefit of these medications: however, well-controlled, scientifically based studies are lacking. The beta-blockers are relatively safe and well-tolerated medications, but the presence of some medical conditions may represent contraindications to their use (such as asthma, sugar diabetes, some heart problems, and others). Side effects can include low blood pressure, heart rate and rhythm changes, nausea, diarrhea, and other gastrointestinal problems, lightheadedness, fatigue and weakness, and depression. The case reports suggest that very high doses of the medications may be necessary, so careful monitoring is important during treatment, especially of blood pressure and heart function.

Stimulants

Because of the frequent occurrence of hyperactivity, impulsivity, and attention deficits among children with autism, the stimulant medications (such as methylphenidate, Ritalin, and others) are often prescribed. This usually occurs during early childhood when autism is sometimes confused with attention deficit hyperactivity disorder. When used in conjunction with educational and behavioral strategies, the stimulants are often highly effective in the treatment of physiologically based attention deficit hyperactivity disorders. However, research and clinical experience suggest that stimulants are not tolerated well by many children with autism. Sedation and an increase in social withdrawal and motor stereotypies may occur. There have been some recent reports that suggest stimulants may be helpful for some hyperactive children with autism, particularly those who are more verbal, intellectually competent, and socially responsive than average. These findings are controversial at present and much more research is needed.

A number of other medications not listed above have been used at one time or another with children or adults with autism. These other medications have been used infrequently and their efficacy remains unproven at this time.

Summary

Psychotropic medications can play an important role in the overall educational and behavioral programming of children and adults with autism. Although there are no known medications that can "cure" the basic dysfunctions associated with the syndrome of autism, the use of medication can help ameliorate a variety of distressing affective and behavioral symptoms that interfere with optimal growth and development. Careful medical and neuropsychiatric assessments are necessary both prior to, and during, treatment so that appropriate medication choices can be made, clinical responses recorded, and side effects monitored. It is very helpful if the physician could be included as an active member of the program-planning team.

Clearly, our present level of knowledge and understanding of this as well as many other areas of autism remain limited, making continued research most important.

Further Information

For additional reading on the subject of medication and autism, see the References section of this book.

Conclusion

This book has been a journey through the sometimes convoluted and confusing highways and byways of the syndrome of autism. While much has been learned about autism and the needs of the children and adults with autism over the past thirty years, so much is still a mystery. I expect that the syndrome will continue to be mysterious and puzzling for the rest of my lifetime.

These unknowns should not blind us to the tremendous progress that has been made in services for people with autism and their families. Most of this progress has been forced through a reluctant human service system by thousands of parents and brothers and sisters of people with autism. The contribution of professionals in many different fields including education, behavior modification, psychiatry and medicine, social work, psychology, counseling, and other fields has done much to improve the lives of many people with autism. Yet we cannot also ignore the history of professional arrogance and ignorance about autism that succeeded in placing burdens of blame and guilt on parents and family members who were already struggling to do their best in often impossible situations. I wish I could say this professional arrogance and ignorance has disappeared, but that is not so.

Probably the most important discovery in all the research discussed in this book is that people with autism are people first; they have individual talents and weaknesses, needs, hopes, and desires, just like anyone else. Families of children and adults with autism are also individual in their coping resources and needs. This individuality means that people with autism and their families need other ordinary people to treat them as members of the local community, invite them out to dinner, work with them in all kinds of job sites. Professionals in the field of autism have an important role to play, but we are learning more and more about the crucial need for people with autism and their families to have friends, neighbors, and relatives who are willing to help out or just listen when needed, and who are in turn willing to be helped themselves.

I do not want to imply that the myriad problems that can be associated with the syndrome of autism can simply be resolved by a lot of warm feelings. There will always be times of despair as well as hope, of sliding backwards as well as making progress, and when there is progress it is often so small that it appears not to be worth the effort to those who do not understand autism. There will always be a need for well-designed research, good technical and professional skills, and people who say "prove it" when we come up with a new approach or technique that is supposed to make a difference. It is important to know what you are doing when you intervene in the lives of people with autism and their families, to be able to say, "I don't know," and to learn all that you can about autism and realize how much still is left unknown.

But the most basic qualification for working with a person with autism or a family is the ability to see the individual not just a syndrome, a willingness to listen, learn, make mistakes then correct the mistakes, and a recognition of how exciting and full of potential every single human life can be.

References

Chapter 1: Basic Questions about Autism

Anderson, G. M., and Y. Hoshino. 1987. "Neurochemical Studies of Autism." In D. J. Cohen and A. M. Donnellan, eds. *Handbook of Autism and Pervasive Developmental Disorders* (pp. 166–91). New York: John Wiley.

Autism Society of North Carolina. 1989. *Autism Primer.* Raleigh.

Blake, A. 1989. "Real Rain Men: The Mystery of the Savant." *Autism Research Review International, 3,* 1–7.

Cohen, D. J., R. Paul, and F. R. Volkmar. 1987. "Issues in the Classification of Pervasive Developmental Disorders and Associated Conditions." In Cohen and Donnellan, *Handbook* (pp. 20–40).

DeMeyer, M. K. 1985. "Research in Infantile Autism: A Strategy and Its Results." In A. M. Donnellan, *Classic Readings in Autism* (pp. 260–80). New York: Teachers College Press.

Donnellan, A. M., and P. L. Mirenda. 1984. "Issues Related to Professional Involvement with Families of Individuals with Autism and Other Severe Handicaps." *Journal of the Association for Persons with Severe Handicaps, 9,* 16–24.

Dreier, P. A. Feb. 19, 1989. "Rain Boy." *New York Times,* p. 28.

Everard, P. 1987. "An International Perspective." In Cohen and Donnellan, *Handbook* (pp. 743–48).

Golden, G. 1987. "Neurological Functioning." In Cohen and Donnellan, *Handbook* (pp. 133–47).

Groden, J., and G. Groden. 1985. "Commentary." In Donnellan, *Classic Readings* (p. 342).

Kanner, L. 1985. "Autistic Disturbances of Affective Contact." In Donnellan, *Classic Readings* (pp. 11–50).

Kilman, B., and N. Negri-Shoultz. 1987. "Developing Educational Programs for Working with Students with Kanner's Autism." In Cohen and Donnellan, *Handbook* (pp. 440–51).

Krug, D. A., J. R. Arick, and P. J. Almond. 1980. *Autism Screening Instrument for Educational Planning.* Portland, OR: ASIEP Educational Co.

Lerea, L. E. 1987. "The Behavioral Assessment of Autistic Children." In Cohen and Donnellan, *Handbook* (pp. 273–88).

Mesibov, G. B., E. Schopler, and W. Caison. 1989. "The Adolescent and Adult Psychoeducational Profile: Assessment of Adolescents and Adults with Severe Developmental Handicaps." *Journal of Autism and Developmental Disorders, 19,* 33–40.

Ornitz, E. M. 1987. "Neurophysiologic Studies of Infantile Autism." In Cohen and Donnellan, *Handbook* (pp. 148–65).

Paul, R. 1987. "Natural History." In Cohen and Donnellan, *Handbook* (pp. 121–30).

Schopler, E., R. J. Reichler, and B. R. Renner. 1986. *The Childhood Autism Rating Scale (CARS).* New York: Irvington.

Sigman, M., J. A. Ungerer, P. Mundy, and T. Sherman. 1987. "Cognition in Autistic Children." Cohen and Donnellan, *Handbook* (pp. 103–20).

Sugiyama, T., and T. Abe. 1989. "The Prevalence of Autism in Nagoya, Japan: A Total Population Study." *Journal of Autism and Developmental Disorders, 19,* 87–96.

Sullivan, R. C. 1987. "Services after 20 Years of Advocacy: A Veteran Parent-Professional's Perspective." In Cohen and Donnellan, *Handbook* (pp. 735–42).

Teal, M. B., and M. J. Wiebe. 1986. "A Validity Analysis of Selected Instruments Used to Assess Autism." *Journal of Autism and Developmental Disorders, 16,* 485–94.

Wing, L., and A. Attwood. 1987. "Syndromes of Autism and Atypical Development." In Cohen and Donnellan, *Handbook* (pp. 3–19).

Wing, L., J. Gould, S. R. Yeates and L. M. Brierley. 1985. "Symbolic Play in Severely Mentally Retarded and in Autistic Children." In Donnellan, *Classic Readings* (pp. 327–341).

Zahner, G. E. P., and D. L. Pauls. 1987. "Epidemiological Surveys of Infantile Autism." In Cohen and Donnellan, *Handbook* (pp. 199–207).

Chapter 2: The Autism Wars: A Brief History of a Controversial Diagnosis

Bettelheim, B. 1967. *The Empty Fortress.* New York: Free Press.

DeMyer, M. K. 1985. "Research in Infantile Autism: A Strategy and Its Results." In Donnellan, *Classic Readings* (pp. 260–80).

Donnellan, A. M. 1985. "Introduction." In Donnellan, *Classic Readings* (pp. 1–10).

Everard, P. 1987. "An International Perspective." In Cohen and Donnellan, *Handbook* (pp. 743–48).

Ferster, C. B. 1985. "Positive Reinforcement and Behavioral Deficits of Autistic Children." In Donnellan, *Classic Readings* (pp. 53–72).

Kanner, L. 1985a. "Autistic Disturbances of Affective Contact." In Donnellan, *Classic Readings* (pp. 11–50).

Kanner, L. 1985b. "Follow-up Study of Eleven Autistic Children Originally Reported in 1943." In Donnellan, *Classic Readings* (pp. 223–34).

LaVigna, G. W. 1985. "Commentary." In Donnellan, *Classic Readings* (p. 73).

Lovaas, O. I., R. Koegel, J. Q. Simmons, and J. S. Long. 1973. "Some Generalizations and Follow-up Measures on Autistic Children in Behavior Therapy." *Journal of Applied Behavior Analysis, 6,* 131–66.

McCarthy, P., K. W. Fender, and D. Fender. 1988. "Supported Employment for Persons with Autism." In P. Wehman and M. S. Moon, eds. *Vocational Rehabilitation and Supported Employment* (pp. 269–90). Baltimore: Brookes Publishing.

Riddle, M. A. 1987. "Individual and Parental Psychotherapy in Autism." In Cohen and Donnellan, *Handbook* (pp. 528–41).

Rimland, B. P. 1964. *Infantile Autism.* New York: Appleton-Century-Crofts.

Rutter, M. 1985. "Commentary." In Donnellan, *Classic Readings* (pp. 50–52).

Schopler, E., and R. J. Reichler. 1971. "Parents as Co-Therapists in the Treatment of Psychotic Children." *Journal of Autism and Childhood Schizophrenia, 1,* p. 87.

Warren, F. 1978. "A Society That Is Going to Kill Your Children." In A. P. Turnbull and H. R. Turnbull III, eds. *Parents Speak Out. Views from the Other Side of the Two-Way Mirror* (pp. 177–96). Columbus, OH: Merrill.

Warren, F. 1987. "Advocacy and Lobbying: Strategies and Techniques for Obtaining Services and Influencing Policy for People with Autism." In Cohen and Donnellan, *Handbook* (pp. 643–52).

Wehman, P. 1988. "Supported Employment. Toward Zero Exclusion of Persons with Severe Disabilities." In Wehman and Moon, *Vocational Rehabilitation* (pp. 3–14).

Chapter 3: A Free, Appropriate Public Education

Bickel, W. E., and D. D. Bickel. 1986. "Effective Schools, Classrooms, and Instruction: Implications for Special Education." *Exceptional Children, 52,* 489–500.

DeRisi, W., and G. Butz. 1975. *Writing Behavioral Contracts.* Champaign, IL: Research Press.

Donnellan, A. M., 1987. "Issues in Developing Personnel Preparation Programs." In Cohen and Donnellan, *Handbook* (pp. 452–75).

Donnellan, A. M., and R. S. Neel. 1986. "New Directions in Educating Students with Autism." In R. H. Horner, L. H. Meyer, and H. D. B. Fredericks, eds. *Education of Learners with Severe Handicaps. Exemplary Service Strategies* (pp. 99–126). Baltimore: Brookes.

Evans, I. M., and L. H. Meyer. 1985. *An Educative Approach to Behavior Problems.* Baltimore: Brookes.

Fischer, J. 1978. *Effective Casework Practice. An Eclectic Approach.* New York: McGraw-Hill.

Florian, L. D., and J. West. 1989. "Congress Affirms the Rights of Children with Handicaps." *Teaching Exceptional Children, 21* (4), 4–7.

Gaylord-Ross, R., K. Stremel-Campbell, and K. Storey. 1986. "Social Skill Training in Natural Contexts." In Horner, Meyer, and Fredericks, *Education of Learners* (pp. 161–87).

Glasser, W. 1975. *Reality Therapy: A New Approach to Psychiatry.* New York: Harper and Row.

Johnson, J., and R. Koegel. 1982. "Behavioral Assessment and Curriculum Development." In R. L. Koegel, A. Rincover, and A. L. Egel, eds. *Educating and Understanding Autistic Children* (pp. 1–32). San Diego: College Hill Press.

Kilman, B., and N. Negri-Shoultz. 1987. "Developing Educational Programs for Working with Students with Kanner's Autism," In Cohen and Donnellan, *Handbook* (pp. 440–51).

Koegel, R. L., A. Rincover, and D. C. Russo. 1982. "Classroom Management: Progression from Special to Normal Classrooms." In Koegel, Rincover, and Egel, *Educating and Understanding* (pp. 203–41).

Lutzker, J., R. V. Campbell, M. Newman, and M. Harrold. 1989. "Ecobehavioral Interventions for Abusive, Neglectful and High-Risk Families." In G. H. S. Singer and L. K. Irvin, eds. *Support for Caregiving Families* (pp. 313–26). Baltimore: Brookes.

Marcus, L., M. Lansing, C. Andrews, and E. Schopler. 1978. "Improvement of Teaching Effectiveness in Parents of Autistic Children." *Journal of the American Academy of Child Psychiatry, 17,* 625–39.

Mesibov, G. B., E. Schopler, B. Schaffer, and R. Landrus. 1988. *Individualized Assessment and Treatment for Autistic and Developmentally Disabled Children: Volume 4, Adolescent and Adult Psychoeducational Profile (AAPEP).* Austin, TX: Pro-Ed.

Mirenda, P. L., and A. M. Donnellan. 1987. "Issues in Curriculum Development." In Cohen and Donnellan, *Handbook* (pp. 211–26).

Olley, J. G. 1987. "Classroom Structure and Autism." In Cohen and Donnellan, *Handbook* (pp. 411–17).

Rose, S. D. 1977. *Group Therapy: A Behavioral Approach.* Englewood Cliffs, NJ: Prentice-Hall.

Rosenberg, N. S. 1987. "Obtaining Educational Services for Autistic Children." In Cohen and Donnellan, *Handbook* (pp. 615–24).

Schopler, E., and R. J. Reichler. 1979. *Individualized Assessment and Treatment for Autistic and Developmentally Disabled Children: Vol. 1 Psychoeducational profile (PEP).* Austin, TX: Pro-Ed.

Schulz, J. 1978. "The Parent-Professional Conflict." In Turnbull and Turnbull, *Parents Speak Out* (pp. 28–37).

Scott, B. S., and J. E. Gilliam. 1987. "Curriculum as a Behavior Management Tool for Students with Autism." *Focus on Autistic Behavior, 2* (1), 1–8.

Simonson, L. R. 1979. *A Curriculum Model for Individuals with Severe Learning and Behavior Disorders.* Baltimore: University Park Press.

Warren, F. 1987. "Advocacy and Lobbying: Strategies and Techniques for Obtaining Services and Influencing Policy for People with Autism." In Cohen and Donnellan, *Handbook* (pp. 643–52).

Zigmond, N., and S. E. Miller. 1986. "Assessment for Instructional Planning." *Exceptional Children, 52,* 501–9.

Chapter 4: Working with Families

Benson, H. A., and A. P. Turnbull. 1986. "Approaching Families from an Individualized Perspective." In Horner, Meyer, and Fredericks, eds. *Education of Learners* (pp. 127–60).

Bristol, M. M., and J. J. Gallagher. 1986. "Research on Fathers of Young Handicapped Children" Evolution, Review and Some Future Directions." In J. J. Gallagher and P. M. Vietze, eds. *Families of Handicapped Persons. Research, Programs and Policy Issues* (pp. 81–100). Baltimore: Brookes.

Cutler, B. C., and M. A. Kozloff. 1987. "Living with Autism: Effects on Families and Family Needs." In Cohen and Donnellan, *Handbook* (pp. 513–27).

Donnellan, A. M., and P. L. Mirenda. 1984. "Issues Related to Professional Involvement with Families of Individuals with

Autism and Other Severe Handicaps." *Journal of the Association for Persons with Severe Handicaps, 9,* 16–24.

Dunst, C. J., C. M. Trivette, N. J. Gordon, and L. L. Pletcher. 1989. "Building and Mobilizing Informal Family Support Networks." In Singer and Irvin, eds. *Support for Caregiving Families* (pp. 121–42).

Hamlin, E. R., and E. M. Timberlake. 1981. "Sibling Group Treatment." *Clinical Social Work Journal, 9,* 101–10.

Hemsley, R., P. Howlin, M. Berger, L. Hersov, D. Holbrook, M. Rutter, and W. Yule. 1978. "Treating Autistic Children in a Family Context." In M. Rutter and E. Schopler, eds. *Autism. A Reappraisal of Concepts and Treatment* (pp. 379–412). New York: Plenum.

Kanner, L. 1985. "Follow-up Study of Eleven Autistic Children Originally Reported in 1943." In Donnellan, *Classic Readings* (pp. 210–58).

Koegel, R. L., L. Schriebman, K. R. Britten, J. C. Burke, and R. E. O'Neill. 1982. "A Comparison of Parent Training to Direct Child Treatment." In Koegel, Rincover, and Egel, *Educating and Understanding* (pp. 260–79).

Lutzker, J., R. V. Campbell, M. Newman, and M. Harrold. 1989. "Ecobehavioral Interventions for Abusive, Neglectful, and High-Risk Families." In G. H. S. Singer and L. K. Irvin, eds. *Support for Caregiving Families. Enabling Positive Adaptation to Disability* (pp. 313–26).

Marcus, L. M., and E. Schopler. 1987. "Working with Families: A Developmental Perspective." In Cohen and Donnellan, *Handbook* (pp. 499–512).

Plienis, A. J., F. R. Robbins, and G. Dunlap. 1988. "Parent Adjustment and Family Stress as Factors in Behavioral Parent Training for Young Autistic Children." *Journal of the Multihandicapped Person, 1,* 31–52.

Roos, P. 1978. "Parents of Mentally Retarded Children—Misunderstood and Mistreated." In Turnbull and Turnbull, *Parents Speak Out* (pp. 12–27).

Schopler, E. 1978. "Changing Parental Involvement in Behavioral Treatment." In M. Rutter and E. Schopler, eds. *Autism.*

A Reappraisal of Concepts and Treatment (pp. 413–21). New York: Plenum.

Simeonsson, R. J., and D. B. Bailey, Jr. 1986. "Siblings of Handicapped Children." In Gallagher and Vietze, *Families of Handicapped Persons* (pp. 67–77).

Strain, P. S., and S. L. Odom. 1986. "Innovations in the Education of Preschool Children with Severe Handicaps." In Horner, Meyer, and Fredericks, *Education of Learners* (pp. 61–98).

Sullivan, R. C. 1979. "Siblings of Autistic Children." *Journal of Autism and Developmental Disorders, 9,* 287–98.

Summers, J. A., S. K. Behr, and A. P. Turnbull. 1989. "Positive Adaptation and Coping Strengths of Families Who Have Children with Disabilities." In Singer and Irvin, *Support for Caregiving Families* (pp. 27–40).

Turnbull, A. P. 1978. "Moving from Being a Professional to Being a Parent: A Startling Experience." In Turnbull and Turnbull, *Parents Speak Out* (pp. 130–40).

Wolf, L. C., S. Noh, S. N. Fisman, and M. Speechley. 1989. "Psychological Effects of Parenting Stress on Parents of Autistic Children." *Journal of Autism and Developmental Disorders, 19.* 157–66.

Yuker, H. E. 1988. "Perceptions of Severely and Multiply Disabled Persons." *Journal of the Multihandicapped Person, 1,* 5–16.

Chapter 5: Working with Adolescents

Agosta, J. 1989. "Using Cash Assistance to Support Family Efforts." In Singer and Irvin, *Support for Caregiving Families* (pp. 189–204).

Bellamy, G. T., L. E. Rhodes, D. M. Mank, and J. M. Albin. 1988. "Parents, Advocates and Friends. Personal Strategies to Foster Supported Employment." In G. T. Bellamy, L. E. Rhodes, D. M. Mank, and J. M. Albin, eds. *Supported Employment. A Community Implementation Guide* (pp. 209–28). Baltimore: Brookes.

Ford, A. 1987. "Sex Education for Individuals with Autism: Structuring Information and Opportunities." In Cohen and Donnellan, *Handbook* (pp. 430–39).

Halvorsen, A. T., K. Doering, F. Farron-Davis, R. Usilton, and W. Sailor. 1989. "The Role of Parents and Family Members in Planning Severely Disabled Students' Transitions from School." In Singer and Irvin, *Support for Caregiving Families* (pp. 253–67).

Lettick, A. L. 1987. "Educational and Residential Placement: Difficulties, Decisions and Issues." In Cohen and Donnellan, *Handbook* (pp. 722–34).

Marcus, L. M., and E. Schopler. 1987. "Working with Families: A Developmental Perspective." In Cohen and Donnellan, *Handbook* (pp. 499–512).

Melone, M., and A. L. Lettick. 1983. "Sex Education at Benhaven." In E. Schopler and G. Mesibov, eds. *Autism in Adolescents and Adults* (pp. 169–86). New York: Plenum.

Paul, R. 1987. "Natural History." In Cohen and Donnellan, *Handbook* (pp. 121–30).

Turnbull III, H. R., A. P. Turnbull, G. B. Bronicki, J. A. Summers, and C. Roeder-Gordon. 1989. *Disability and the Family. A Guide to Decisions for Adulthood.* Baltimore: Brookes.

Wilcox, B., J. J. McDonnell, G. T. Bellamy, and H. Rose. 1988. "Preparing for Supported Employment: The Role of Secondary Special Education." In Bellamy, Rhodes, Mank, and Albin, *Supported Employment* (pp. 183–208).

Chapter 6: Adults with Autism

Apolloni, T. 1989. "Guardianship, Trusts, and Protective Services." In Singer and Irvin, *Support for Caregiving Families* (pp. 283–96).

Kilman, B., and N. Negri-Shoultz. 1987. "Developing Educational Programs for Working with Students with Kanner's Autism." In Cohen and Donnellan, *Handbook* (pp. 440–51).

Marcus, L. M., and E. Schopler. 1987. "Working with Families: A Developmental Perspective." In Cohen and Donnellan, *Handbook* (pp. 499–512).

McCarthy, P., K. W. Fender, and D. Fender. 1988. "Supported Employment for Persons with Autism." In Wehman and Moon, *Vocational Rehabilitation* (pp. 269–90).

Meichenbaum, D. 1975. "Self-instructional Methods." In F. H. Kanfer and A. P. Goldstein, eds. *Helping People Change* (pp. 357–91). New York: Pergamon.

Paul, R. 1987. "Natural History." In Cohen and Donnellan, *Handbook* (pp. 121–30).

Riddle, M. A. 1987. "Individual and Parental Psychotherapy in Autism." In Cohen and Donnellan, *Handbook* (pp. 528–41).

Schopler, E., and G. Mesibov. 1983. *Autism in Adolescents and Adults.* New York: Plenum.

Sullivan, R. C. 1987. "Services after 20 Years of Advocacy: A Parent-Professional's Perspective." In Cohen and Donnellan, *Handbook* (pp. 735–42).

Turnbull III, H. R., A. P. Turnbull, G. J. Bronicki, J. A. Summers, and C. Roeder-Gordon. 1989. *Disability and the Family. A Guide to Decisions for Adulthood.* Baltimore: Brookes.

Chapter 7: Medication

Campbell, M., L. T. Anderson, W. H. Green, and S. I. Deutsch. 1987. "Psychopharmacology." In Cohen and Donnellan, *Handbook* (pp. 545–65).

duVerglas, G., S. R. Banks, and K. E. Guyer. 1988. "Clinical Effects of Fenfluramine on Children with Autism: A Review of the Research." *Journal of Autism and Developmental Disorders, 18,* 297–308.

Mikkelson, E. 1982. "Efficacy of Neuroleptic Medication in Pervasive Developmental Disorders of Childhood." *Schizophrenia Bulletin, 8,* 320–32.

THE CONTINUUM
COUNSELING LIBRARY
Books of Related Interest

————Denyse Beaudet
ENCOUNTERING THE MONSTER
Pathways in Children's Dreams
Based on original empirical research, and with recourse to the
works of Jung, Neumann, Eliade, Marie-Louise Franz, and
others, this book offers proven methods of approaching and
understanding the dream life of children. $17.95

————Robert W. Buckingham
CARE OF THE DYING CHILD
A Practical Guide for Those Who Help Others
"Buckingham's book delivers a powerful, poignant message
deserving a wide readership."—*Library Journal* $17.95

————Alastair V. Campbell, ed.
A DICTIONARY OF PASTORAL CARE
Contains over 300 entries by 185 authors in the fields of
theology, philosophy, psychology, and sociology as well as
from psychotherapy and counseling. $24.50

————David A. Crenshaw
BEREAVEMENT
Counseling the Grieving throughout the Life Cycle
Grief is examined from a life cycle perspective, infancy to old
age. Special losses and practical strategies for frontline
caregivers highlight this comprehensive guidebook. $17.95

————H. J. Eysenck, W. Arnold, and R. Meili, eds.
ENCYCLOPEDIA OF PSYCHOLOGY
Covering all aspects of psychology, this book features brief
definitions and essays by subject specialists.
"An authoritative reference book in a clear and intelligible
language. Essential."—*Booklist* $60.00

————Reuben Fine
THE HISTORY OF PSYCHOANALYSIS
New Expanded Edition
"Objective, comprehensive, and readable. A rare work.
Highly recommended, whether as an introduction to the field
or as a fresh overview to those already familiar with it."
—*Contemporary Psychology* $24.95 (paperback)

————Lucy Freeman
FIGHT AGAINST FEARS
With a new Introduction by Flora Rheta Schreiber
More than a million copies sold; the new—and only
available—edition of the first, and still best, true story of a
modern woman's journey of self-discovery through
psychoanalysis. $10.95

————Lucy Freeman
OUR INNER WORLD OF RAGE
Understanding and Transforming the Power of Anger
A psychoanalytic examination of the anger that burns within
us and which can be used to save or slowly destroy us. Sheds
light on all expressions of rage, from the murderer to the
suicide to those of us who feel depressed and angry but are
unaware of the real cause. $15.95

————Lucy Freeman and Kerstin Kupfermann
THE POWER OF FANTASY
Where Our Daydreams Come From, and How They Can Help or Harm Us
This is the first book to explain the role of both daydreams and unconscious fantasies in our lives, helping us to distinguish between those that can unleash our creativity and those that can emotionally cripple us. $16.95

————John Gerdtz and Joel Bregman, M.D.
AUTISM
A Practical Guide for Those Who Help Others
An up-to-date and comprehensive guidebook for everyone who works with autistic children, adolescents, adults, and their families. Includes latest information on medications. $17.95

————Marion Howard
HOW TO HELP YOUR TEENAGER
POSTPONE SEXUAL INVOLVEMENT
Based on a national educational program that works, this book advises parents, teachers, and counselors on how they can help their teens resist social and peer pressures regarding sex. $14.95

————Marion Howard
SOMETIMES I WONDER ABOUT ME
Teenagers and Mental Health
Combines fictional narratives with sound, understandable professional advice to help teenagers recognize the difference between serious problems and normal problems of adjustment. $9.95

————E. Clay Jorgensen
CHILD ABUSE
A Practical Guide for Those Who Help Others
Essential information and practical advice for caregivers called upon to help both child and parent in child abuse. $16.95

————Eugene Kennedy
CRISIS COUNSELING
The Essential Guide for Nonprofessional Counselors
"An outstanding author of books on personal growth selects
types of personal crises that our present life-style has made
commonplace and suggests effective ways to deal with
them."—*Best Sellers* $11.95

————Eugene Kennedy and Sara C. Charles, M.D.
ON BECOMING A COUNSELOR
A Basic Guide for Nonprofessional Counselors
New expanded edition of an indispensable resource. A
patient-oriented, clinically directed field guide to
understanding and responding to troubled people.
$27.95 hardcover $15.95 paperback

————Eugene Kennedy
SEXUAL COUNSELING
A Practical Guide for Those Who Help Others
Newly revised and up-to-date edition of an essential book on
counseling people with sexual problems, with a new chapter
on AIDS. $17.95

————Bonnie Lester
WOMEN AND AIDS
A Practical Guide for Those Who Help Others
Provides positive ways for women to deal with their fears, and
to help others who react with fear to people who have AIDS.
$15.95

————Helen B. McDonald and Audrey I. Steinhorn
HOMOSEXUALITY
*A Practical Guide to Counseling Lesbians, Gay Men, and Their
Families*
A sensitive guide to better understanding and counseling gays,
lesbians, and their parents, at every stage of their lives. $16.95

————Janice N. McLean and Sheila A. Knights
PHOBICS AND OTHER PANIC VICTIMS
A Practical Guide for Those Who Help Them
"A must for the phobic, spouse, and family, and for the
physician and support people who help them. It can spell the
difference between partial therapy with partial results and
comprehensive therapy and recovery."—Arthur B. Hardy,
M.D., Founder, TERRAP Phobia Program, and Past
President, Phobia Society of America $17.95

————Cherry Boone O'Neill
DEAR CHERRY
Questions and Answers on Eating Disorders
Practical and inspiring advice on eating disorders from the
best-selling author of *Starving for Attention.* $8.95

————Paul G. Quinnett
ON BECOMING A HEALTH AND HUMAN SERVICES
MANAGER
A Practical Guide for Clinicians and Counselors
A new and essential guide to management for everyone in the
helping professions—from mental health to nursing, from
social work to teaching. $19.95

————Paul G. Quinnett
SUICIDE: THE FOREVER DECISION
For Those Thinking About Suicide, and for Those Who Know, Love,
or Counsel Them
"A treasure—this book can help save lives. It will be especially
valuable not only to those who are thinking about suicide but
to such nonprofessional counselors as teachers, clergy,
doctors, nurses, and to experienced therapists."
—William Van Ornum, psychotherapist and author
$18.95 hardcover $8.95 paperback

————Paul G. Quinnett
THE TROUBLED PEOPLE BOOK
A practical and positive guide to the world of psychotherapy and psychotherapists. "Without a doubt one of the most honest, reassuring, nonpaternalistic, and useful self-help books ever to appear."—*Booklist* $9.95

————Judah L. Ronch
ALZHEIMER'S DISEASE
A Practical Guide for Those Who Help Others
Must reading for everyone—from family members to professional caregivers—who must deal with the effects of this tragic disease on a daily basis. Filled with illustrative examples as well as facts, this book provides sensitive insights into dealing with one's feelings as well as with such practical advice as how to choose long-term care. $17.95

————Theodore Isaac Rubin, M.D.
ANTI-SEMITISM: A DISEASE OF THE MIND
"A most poignant and lucid psychological examination of a severe emotional disease. Dr. Rubin offers hope and understanding to the victim and to the bigot. A splendid job!"—Dr. Herbert S. Strean $14.95

————John R. Shack
COUPLES COUNSELING
A Practical Guide for Those Who Help Others
An essential guide to dealing with the 20 percent of all counseling situations that involve the relationship of two people. $17.95

————Stuart Sutherland
THE INTERNATIONAL DICTIONARY OF PSYCHOLOGY
This new dictionary of psychology also covers a wide range of related disciplines, from anthropology to sociology. $49.95

————Joan Leslie Taylor
IN THE LIGHT OF DYING
The Journals of a Hospice Volunteer
A rare and beautiful book about death and dying that affirms
life and will inspire an attitude of love. "Beautifully recounts
the healing (our own) that results from service to others, and
might well be considered as required reading for hospice
volunteers."—Stephen Levine $17.95

————Montague Ullman, M.D. and Claire Limmer, eds.
THE VARIETY OF DREAM EXPERIENCE
Expanding Our Ways of Working with Dreams
"Lucidly describes the beneficial impact dream analysis can
have in diverse fields and in society as a whole. An erudite,
illuminating investigation."—*Booklist* $19.95 hardcover $14.95
paperback

————William Van Ornum and John Mordock
CRISIS COUNSELING WITH CHILDREN AND
ADOLESCENTS
"It's the kind of book every parent should keep on the shelf
next to nutrition, medical, and Dr. Spock books."—*Marriage
& Family Living* $12.95

————William Van Ornum and Mary W. Van Ornum
TALKING TO CHILDREN ABOUT NUCLEAR WAR
"A wise book. A needed book. An urgent book."—Dr.
Karl A. Menninger $15.95 hardcover $7.95 paperback

At your bookstore, or to order directly, send your check or
money order (adding $2.00 extra per book for postage and
handling, up to $6.00 maximum) to: The Continuum Publishing
Company, 370 Lexington Avenue, New York, NY 10017. Prices
are subject to change.